THE GREAT AND THE GOOD
An Inquiry into the British Establishment

Research Report No: 654 (March 1986)

PETER HENNESSY

D1375745

Policy Studies Institute

Hennessy, Peter, 1947 –
The great and the good: an inquiry into the British establishment.
– (Research report; 654)
1. Governmental investigations – Great Britain
I. Title   II. Series
354.4109'3   KD4895

ISBN 0-85374-272-3

Published by Policy Studies Institute
100 Park Village East, London NW1 3SR
Printed by Bourne Offset Ltd.

Peter Brookes' caricature of the Falkland Islands Review Committee, 1982-83.
From left to right, Mr Merlyn Rees, Lord Carrington (witness not committee
member), Lord Barber, Sir Patrick Nairne, Lord Franks, Lord Lever and Lord
Watkinson.
Mr Brookes' conception of the British Establishment is emblazoned on the briefcase
on the cover.

Reproduced by kind permission of the cartoonist.

PREFACE

THE ESTABLISHMENT NOTION

FINDING THE GREAT AND THE GOOD

A TRIO OF GRANDEES

CRITICISM AND DECLINE

TOWARDS A NOUVEAU REGIME

APPENDIX ONE: ROYAL COMMISSIONS AND COMMITTEES OF INQUIRY, 1945-85

APPENDIX TWO: NEW STARTS, 1945-85

APPENDIX THREE: CABINET OFFICE PUBLIC APPOINTMENTS UNIT SELF-NOMINATION FORM

PREFACE

Once, when Giant Reason still ruled in old England, they used an archaic device, called a Royal Commission or a Committee of Inquiry.
Professor Peter Hall, 1985(1)

There is a fashion in these things and when you are in fashion you get asked to do a lot.
Lord Franks, 1977(2)

Committees are the oriflamme of democracy.
Harold Macmillan, 1953(3)

When William the Conqueror decided, while spending his Christmas holiday at Gloucester in 1085, to assess the national income of his kingdom, he started something. The noblemen he despatched as commissioners to do the work - men like Remigius, the Bishop of Lincoln, and the Barons Henry de Ferrers and Walter Giffard(4) - were the prototype Great and Good of old England and the Domesday Book of 1086 was their first report. This study is a Nine Hundredth Anniversary tribute to a great British institution which is currently enduring what will probably be a temporary eclipse.

My thanks are due to Anthony Sampson for giving me, while I was still at grammar school, an appreciation of the importance of committees and committee men in public life(5); to Sir William Rees-Mogg, Harold Evans and the late Charles Douglas-Home, successive editors of The Times, who allowed me to indulge my fascination for the world of the Great and the Good in the columns of their newspapers; to Anne Winder, a gem amongst producers, who collaborated with me on a BBC Radio 3 documentary on the

1

G and G(6); to George Fischer, Head of Talks and Documentaries, Radio, who commissioned it; to Ian Macintyre, Controller of Radio 3, who allowed it to be broadcast; to the contributors to the programme who coached me in the ways of the G and G, Lord Franks, Lord Bullock, Lady Warnock, Jonathan Charkham, Sir Henry Chilver, Professor Ralf Dahrendorf, Lord Donoughue, Sir Reginald Hibbert, Dr David Owen, Sir Anthony Parsons, Clive Priestley and Dr Bernard Williams; to Gus Macdonald for inviting me to examine the broadcasting branch of the G & G; to Robert Ingram of Charterhouse, Dr Christopher Andrew of Corpus Christi College, Cambridge, General Patrick Palmer of the Staff College, Camberley and Dr Jim Sharpe of Nuffield College, Oxford, for allowing me to test my themes in their institutions; to Stephanie Maggin for processing the words; to Peter Brookes for kind permisson to reproduce two of his marvellous cartoons; and finally thanks to my wife Nid, who helped me compile the appendices.

PETER HENNESSY
WALTHAMSTOW AND SOMERS TOWN,
MARCH 1986

Footnotes

(1)   Peter Hall, 'How Other People Run Their Cities', <u>New Society</u>, January 10, 1985, p.44.
(2)   Conversation with Lord Franks, January 24, 1977.
(3)   Public Record Office PREM 11/ 952. C(53)322. Memorandum on Smog by the Minister of Housing and Local Government, November 18, 1953.
(4)   Peter B. Boyden, 'The making of Domesday Book', <u>History Today</u>, Volume 36, January 1986, p.23.
(5)   The volume in question, which I received as a sixth form prize in 1965, was Anthony Sampson, <u>Anatomy of Britain Today</u>, Hodder, 1965. On page 312 Mr Sampson wrote of 'A secret tome of the <u>Great and the Good</u>' which was my first acquaintance with the famous list of the G & G.
(6)   'The Good and the Great' was broadcast on BBC Radio 3 on February 4, 1984. An article based on it - Peter Hennessy, 'The most elevated and distinguished casualties of the Thatcher years' - was published in <u>The Listener</u>, February 7, 1985.

THE ESTABLISHMENT NOTION

Let a fairy grant me my three wishes, I would gladly use them all in one prayer only, that never again should anyone using pen or type writer be permitted to employ that inane cliche 'Establishment'.
Lord Radcliffe, 1961(1)

In truth all organisations and institutions, whether public or private, commerical or charitable, business or academic, paid or voluntary, have an establishment. It consists of those who, within that organisation or institution, are the group which exercise power or influence and, particularly when applied to the public sector, are generally regarded as seeking to resist change.
Sir Frank Cooper, 1986(2)

I loathe the Establishment and always have done. They've never been able to envelop me.
Dr David Owen, 1984(3)

Establishment culture is the culture of sound and comfortable men.
Lord Donoughue, 1984(4)

'The Establishment' is a fluid, mercurial concept, infuriating in its imprecision to minds as tidy as the late Lord Radcliffe's. It was not always so. Lord Radcliffe himself quotes the toast common amongst the rural Anglican clergy in the early nineteenth century - 'Prosperity to the Establishment and confusion to all Enthusiasts'(5). Those sound and comfortable clergy were referring, no doubt, to the Established church, that is, their own, and to the vulgar enthusiasms of the Non-Conformists. But had their targets been secular the toast would have seemed equally apt. For

4

their period was the tail-end of the Whig autocracy when the Establishment knew who it was and the non-Established did, too. They were the Whig grandees, landed men who possessed huge estates and elegant mansions which exuded, as Lord David Cecil put it, 'an extraordinary impression of culture and elegance and established power'(6). For Cecil, the Whig aristocracy:

> was before all other things a governing class. At a time when economic power was concentrated in the landed interest, the Whigs were amongst the biggest landowners; their party was in office for the greater part of the eighteenth century; during this period they possessed a large proportion of the seats in the House of Commons; they produced more ambassadors and officers of state than the rest of England put together. And they lived on a scale appropriate to their power(7).

The eighteenth century Establishment ran England, which was still very largely a patronage society, from those marvellous country estates - 'their houses were alive with the effort and hurry of politics. Red Foreign Office boxes strewed the library tables, at any time of day or night a courier might come galloping up with critical news, and the minister must post off to London to attend a Cabinet meeting'.

The nineteenth century saw a blurring of the boundaries of political and financial power, beneficial, no doubt for the British economy but highly inconvenient for the cartographer of the Establishment. The progressive shift of money and influence from country to city, from agriculture to manufacturing, the blossoming of a professional middle class, their representation in a new kind of politics, led to a seepage of power from those 'cream and gilt libraries piled with sumptuous editions of the classics'(9) and littered with official papers from Whitehall, and its dispersal throughout a thoroughly confusing diaspora which, by Edwardian times, had even begun to embrace the trade union movement.

It is typical of the development of language that the vocabulary of power took about a century to catch up with what by the end of the First World War was a thoroughly faded Whig ascendancy, though the country house phenomenon, its attendant habits and morals, remained quite capable of capturing the politically, socially and economically mobile on their way up. The noun 'establishment' begins to make its sporadic appearance just as the Conservative Party of Stanley Baldwin and the Labour Party of Ramsay MacDonald were about to bury the fragmented husk of the

Old Liberal Party into which the Whigs, with some difficulty, had eventually deliquesced. In 1923, in R. Macaulay's <u>Told by an Idiot</u>, the following sentence appears containing not just <u>that</u> word but an enduring truth as well: 'The moderns of one day become the safe establishments of the next'(10).

But its usage in our time is largely the responsibility of that most diverting and intellectually fertile of postwar political commentators, Henry Fairlie. In his regular 'Political Commentary' column in <u>The Spectator</u> in September 1955, shortly after Guy Burgess and Donald Maclean, the notorious pair of defecting British diplomants, had turned up in Moscow, Fairlie suggested that the 'Establishment' would continue to cover up for two of its own:

> ... what I call the 'Establishment' in this country is today more powerful than ever before. By the 'Establishment' I do not mean only the centres of official power though they are certainly part of it - but rather the whole matrix of official and social relations within which power is excercised.

> ... Somewhere near the heart of the patterns of social relationships which so powerfully controll the exercise of power in this country is the Foreign Office ... At the time of the disappearance of Maclean and Burgess, 'the right people' moved into action ... No one whose job it was to be interested in the Burgess-Maclean affair from the very beginning will forget the subtle but powerful pressures which were brought to bear by those who belonged to the same stratum as the two missing men(11).

Fairlie, for all his excellent contacts, cannot have known just how fully he would be vindicated when papers from Sir Anthony Eden's Cabinet were released under the Thirty Year Rule in January 1986. A combination of the reappearance of Burgess and Maclean and the revelations in Australia of the KGB defector Vladimir Petrov, had created something of a frenzy in Westminster political circles, particularly as Petrov had pointed to the existence of a Third Man who had tipped off B and M that MI5 was closing in. It was clear to ministers that a parliamentary statement would be required promising action of some kind. The Foreign Secretary, Harold Macmillan, was the urbane incarnation of those values, mannerisms and social connections Fairlie had in mind in his article. In a Cabinet Paper circulated on October 19, 1955 Macmillan recoiled from the prospect of a public inquiry for which the Labour Opposition was pressing as 'Nothing could be worse than a lot of muck raking and innuendo. It would be like one of the immense divorce cases which there used to be when I was young, going on for days and days, every detail reported in the press'(12).

He told the Cabinet on October 20, 1955, 'he was concerned that there was nothing to be said for holding an inquest into the past. This would give currency to a stream of false and misleading statements which could never be overtaken and corrected in the public mind'(13). Macmillan favoured instead an internal inquiry into security procedures. The Cabinet concurred and a committee of Privy Counsellors was summoned for the purpose, chaired by Lord Salisbury (see Annex 1). Lack of incriminating evidence obliged Macmillan to clear the name of Kim Philby, the former M16 officer, during the Commons debate that ensued. This later proved embarrassing to Macmillan as Prime Minister in January 1963 when Philby himself defected to Moscow.

Fairlie may not have shamed the Foreign Office into candour in 1955, but he did strike a chord with the more irreverent members of the political nation. The phrase 'Establishment' stuck to an extent which by 1961 had infuriated Lord Radcliffe. Before enumerating Fairlie's followers in the late 1950s, natural justice requires me to risk the charge of unfashionability by claiming that one aspect of Establishment supremacy in Burgess and Maclean territory was probably beneficial. The fact that Britain's cold war security purge of its public service was kept inside the family, as it were, did ensure that we avoided any serious outbreak of home-grown McCarthyism. The occasional oddball, such as Sir Waldron Smithers MP, would regularly press for a Select Committee on Un-British Activities. But the answer, whether it was from Mr Attlee or Mr Churchill, was the same(14). The permanent secretaries, with the backing of ministers, kept tight control over the purge to avoid making martyrs(15). Neither political party sought to make security the kind of issue at the polls it had become in the United States after the 1948 presidential election.

Such a claim in mid-Fifties England would have been dubbed an irredeemable statement of Establishment wisdom and derided accordingly. The names of the dervisors who followed Fairlie make for glittering reading. Lord Altrincham (better known as the journalist and political biographer John Grigg) launched his broadside against the Establishment in National and English Review two years after Fairlie's opening salvo(16). The gilded, through not so youthful, C.P. Snow, in the Conscience of the Rich, published in 1958, referred to 'that gang' by which he meant the people who had the real power, the rulers, the Establishment(17). And in 1959, the year of Macmillan's electoral triumph (though some two years ahead of the satire boom), the Fairlie genre was crowned when Anthony Blond published The Establishment: A Symposium(18) edited by the young Hugh Thomas, a top-flight historian, working at that time at his classic study of The Spanish Civil War(19) after employment as a diplomat in the Foreign Office, and as a lecturer at the Royal Military Acadamy, Sandhurst.

Thomas himself contributed an essay on the class system; the economist John Vaizey opened his discussion with a typically Vaizeyian squib - 'Intelligent discussion of the public schools is handicapped by the fact that they are indescribably funny'(20); the novelist Simon Raven turned his formidable word-power on the military; the economist Thomas Balogh made the most quoted and longest lasting contribution in his famous attack on the senior Civil Service, 'The Apotheosis of the Dilettante'; stockbroker Victor Sandelson dissected the City Establishment; the former Tory MP, Christopher Hollis, tackled 'Parliament and the Establishment'; while founding father, Henry Fairlie, rounded the volume off with an attack on the BBC, 'of all the voices of the Establishment', he wrote, 'the British Broadcasting Corporation is the most powerful'(21).

Three of the contributors were themselves to benefit from what Michael De-La-Noy called 'the establishment bounty'(22) - the honours system. Balogh was created a peer by Harold Wilson as was Vaizey, though he died a convinced supporter of Mrs Thatcher, who ennobled the symposium's editor as Lord Thomas of Swynnerton. Lord Thomas now runs what might be called the Prime Minister's private think tank, the Centre for Policy Studies. Their collective ennoblement might be construed as proof positive of Macaulay's doctrine whereby the moderns of one day became the Establishment of the next though a peerage does not necessarily confer honorary membership of the Establishment. Indeed, only one member of the House of Lords, Lord Franks, is on record as acknowledging his inclusion among its ranks:

> If anybody likes to label me in that way, I don't object, because what it means is that I have done public duties from time to time. That's by definition being a member of the Establishment - so yes(23).

For the purposes of this study, the Franks criterion - that of performing 'public duties from time to time' - is the benchmark to be used for tracing the contours of the Establishment. It cannot be a complete map. Each profession has its own Establishment and not all of those involved engage in wider public duties. Each sport has its own Establishment. Alan Watkins once unforgettably described Mr Peter May, Chairman of the Test Selectors, as 'one of those who view the world from behind a collar-stud'(24). For some it is all a question of political attitudes. Ronald Butt reckons 'the great and the good among political commentators' are those 'whose idea of political neutrality resembles the collected words and deeds of Mr Roy Jenkins and Mrs Shirley Williams', an 'establishment which Mrs Thatcher had the effrontery to challenge with some of the common sense of the suburbs'(25). For others, like Tim Heald, it is a question of networks, clusters of old boy networks to be precise, based on family, school, college, club(26). All this illustrates the impossibility of doing for the contemporary British Establishment what Lord David Cecil did for the Whigs.

The Franks criterion, however, does help to isolate and identify an important and ancient slice of it - the Great and the Good, the men and women whose names are kept on the famous List of the Great and the Good in the Cabinet Office to which ministers and permanent secretaries resort when searching for people to sit on Royal Commissions, committees of inquiry, the boards of nationalised industries plus assorted advisory councils, Britains 'half awake quangoland', as Peter Jenkins rather cruelly characterised it(27). Who are the 'great', who are the 'good'? How are they found? What is their utility? Are they an elite? If so, of what kind - an aristocracy, a gerontocracy, a meritocracy or merely a 'legitimate mafia'(28)? Centenaries are a fitting moment to find out.

Footnotes
(1)   Lord Radcliffe, 'Censors', The Rede Lecture, Cambridge University, May 4, 1961, reproduced in Lord Radcliffe, Not in Feather Beds, Hamish Hamilton, 1968, pp.161-82. This particular quotation is on p.175.
(2)   Sir Frank Cooper, 'Changing the Establishment', L.S.E. Suntary Toyota Lecture, March 12, 1986.
(3)   'The Terry Coleman Interview', The Guardian, September 8, 1984.
(4)   Conversation with Lord Donoughue, November 29, 1984.
(5)   Radcliffe, Feather Beds, p.175.
(6)   David Cecil, The Young Melbourne, Constable, 1939, p.2.
(7)   Ibid., pp.2-3.
(8)   Ibid., p.5.
(9)   Ibid., p.1.

(10) Quoted in Supplement to the Oxford English Dictionary Volume 1, OUP, 1972, p.976.

(11) Henry Fairlie, 'Political Commentary', The Spectator, September 23, 1955, p.380.

(12) Public Record Office CAB 129/78, CP (55) 161, 'Disappearance of two Foreign Office officials, Burgess and Maclean', October 19, 1955.

(13) PRO CAB 128/29, CM (55) 36, October 20, 1955, Item 6.

(14) Peter Hennessy and Gail Brownfeld, 'Britain's Cold War Security Purge: The Origins of Positive Vetting', The Historical Journal, 25,4 (1982) p.965.

(15) Ibid., p.972.

(16) National and English Review, September 10, 1957, p.8.

(17) C.P. Snow, Conscience of the Rich.

(18) Hugh Thomas (editor), The Establishment: A Symposium, Anthony Blond, 1959.

(19) Hugh Thomas, The Spanish Civil War, Harper and Row, 1961.

(20) Ibid., p.23.

(21) Ibid., p.191.

(22) Michael De-La-Noy, 'Arise, Sir...', New Society, January 10, 1986, p.69.

(23) 'The Good and the Great', BBC Radio 3, February 4, 1985.

(24) Alan Watkins, 'Diary', The Spectator, June 15, 1985, p.7.

(25) Ronald Butt, 'Why Mrs Thatcher could win again', The Times, June 20, 1985.

(26) Tim Heald, Networks. Who We Know and How We Use Them, Hodder 1983.

(27) Peter Jenkins, 'The forging of Pym's Rebellion', The Sunday Times, May 12, 1985.

(28) This delightful analogy was made in Richard H-Rovere, The American Establishment And Other Report, Opinions and Speculations, Hart-Davis, 1963, pp.233-4.

FINDING THE GREAT AND THE GOOD

A secret tome of <u>The Great and The Good</u> is kept, listing everyone who has the right, safe qualifications of worthiness, soundness, and discretion; and from this tome come the stage army of committee people.
Anthony Sampson, 1965(1)

Nor ought one exclusively to rely on the Civil Service Department's famous 'List of the Great and Good', all of whose members, if I may be allowed to indulge for a moment in my propensity to exaggerate, are aged fifty-three, live in the South-East, have the right accent and belong to the Reform Club.
Lord Rothschild, 1976(2)

I would welcome new names. I seek new names.
Paul Channon, Minister of State, Civil Service Department, 1980(3)

The origin of the phrase 'the great and the good' is lost in the Establishment mists, though it is highly unlikely that one of their own invented it given its ironic, faintly comical overtones. I encountered it as a child in the 1950s when, in common with thousands of Roman Catholic youths at Benediction, I would trill 'God bless our Pope, the great, the good'. But this is to confuse matters. Whatever the progress of ecumenism, His Holiness will be never be invited to chair a British Royal Commission. The phrase 'great and good' conveys an aura of wisdom and benevolence. Its ambience is apolitical, high-minded, non-partisan. The activity it suggests is one which eschews short term gain for long term benefit, putting the strategic above the tactical.
The 'List of the Great and the Good', however, suggests that a hierarchy exists among committee people in the eyes of ministers

11

and senior civil servants who do the choosing. As Tom Schuller, an Associate Member of Nuffield College, Oxford, has suggested, 'The Great' are the Lord Franks's of this world, people of chairman potential, and 'The Good' are the rest who fill the chairs either side of the green baize tables(4). A month after he uttered it, the Schuller distinction acquired the kind of sanctity that only an official document can confer. At the preview of the 1955 Cabinet papers granted to the press on December 30 and 31, 1985, the story of how the Eden Cabinet authorised the preparation of a draft Commonwealth Immigrants Bill, designed to restrict the inflow of coloured people from the colonies, attracted much attention. Particularly appreciated by journalists at the table around which sat representatives of The Times, The Guardian and New Society was a collector's item which offered a rare insight into the decorous hierarchical world of the Great and Good.

The Home Secretary, Gwilym Lloyd George, a convinced protagonist of control, recognised that parliamentary and public opinion in mid-1955 was not generally aware that unrestricted coloured immigration from the colonies was causing difficulties in certain parts of the inner cities and that the problem would worsen unless curbs were applied on the waterfront and at the airports. As Sir Norman Brook, Secretary of the Cabinet, explained in a steering brief to Sir Anthony Eden, drafted on June 14, 1955, 'the Home Secretary proposes a committee of enquiry. Its purpose would be, not to find a solution (for it is evident what form control must take), but to enlist a sufficient body of public support for the legislation that would be needed'(5). Three days earlier, Lloyd George had circulated a Cabinet Paper suggesting 'the following for the composition of the committee':

Chairman: Lord Radcliffe, or failing him, the Earl of Crawford and Balcarres, or Mr John Sparrow (Warden of All Souls) or Sir David Lindsay Keir (Master of Balliol).
One Conservative, One Labour and One Liberal MP.
One representative of employers' organisations.
One representative of the TUC.
One person familiar with Commonwealth problems, to be nominated by the Commonwealth Secretary.
One person experienced in colonial administration, to be nominated by the Colonial Secretary.
One person (preferably a woman) well known as a social worker.
One economic expert.
One member of a local authority concerned with housing and public health questions.

At least one of the members should be chosen from Scotland and one from Wales(6).

The terms of reference for this committee of 11, chaired by a big name and peopled by a carefully balanced ballast encompassing political parties, capital and labour, relevant experience, a woman and persons from Scotland and Wales, were to be:

> To consider and report whether, having regard to the importance of maintaining traditional ties between this country and other parts of the Commonwealth, any, and if so, what?, changes in the law relating to the admission to the United Kingdom of British subjects from overseas (or any class of them) and to their subsequent stay in the United Kingdom, are necessary or desirable in the national interest and in the interests of the immigrants themselves(7).

Norman Brook, himself an experienced Home Office hand(8), told the Prime Minister 'I think that most members of the Cabinet now agree that a report by an independent committee is necessary for this purpose'(9). But, showing where _real_ patronage lies in the system, he applied a very superior version of quality control to the names dished up by the Home Secretary, confirming in the process, Lord Radcliffe's position as unofficial No. 1 on the List of the Great and Good. Brook wrote to Eden:

> Of the Chairmen suggested, John Sparrow seems the best. Lord Radcliffe, who is in great demand, should be reserved for subjects which are more complex or difficult intellectually. Lord Crawford also would do other things better. John Sparrow is a lawyer: though he is untried, I think, as a committee chairman, it would be quite a good thing to bring him into this sort of work(10).

All Brook's careful sifting came to naught. No committee on coloured immigration was commissioned. Cabinet discussion proved inconclusive and Eden booted the issue into touch by establishing a Cabinet Committee on the subject chaired by Lord Kilmuir, the Lord Chancellor(11). And when Parliament eventually legislated on the matter with the Commonwealth Immigration Act in 1962(12) it did so without the benefit of prior advice from a committee of the great and good.

The reaction of officials involved in the G and G operation in the 1980s to the publication of that 1955 document was two-fold:

13

'nothing changes', said one(13), 'You're very lucky to get that', said another, 'it doesn't very often get on the file'(14). Indeed, the Thirty Year Rule does not seem to apply to the list of the Great and the Good. Its custodians in the Forties and Fifties were part of the Treasury's Establishment side. But no trace of the List or the running files of its compilers have reached the Public Record Office, which means that the systems analyst of the G and G must rely on occasional pieces of flotsam to follow the real power of patronage through its underground channels.

Mercifully, as that anonymous insider put it, 'nothing changes', at the top level at least. There have been important improvements in the engine room, if not on the bridge, since the mid-1970s changes to which we will turn later. What other beams of light exist to illuminate patronage at the top? The ultimate locus of power in No.10 is in fact, laid down in the secret rules of the Cabinet system, the now famous document called Questions of Procedure for Ministers. The relevant paragraph in the most recent version I have seen reads on as follows:

> The Prime Minister should be consulted in advance about appointments of chairmen and deputy chairmen of national-ised industries and public boards; he should be informed in advance of about appointments of chairmen and deputy chairmen of the more important departmental committees of an independent or semi-independent nature; and he should be given the opportunity to comment before the appointment of members of boards and commissions in cases where they are likely to have political significance(15).

The second tier of patronage, one below that of the prime minister, is beautifully laid bare in Mrs Castle's Diary dealing with the period 1974-76 when she was Secretary of State for the Social Services. In 1975, the Wilson government was keen to buy time on the controversial issue of private beds in National Health Service hospitals. The remedy, sanctified by long Wilsonian practice, was to establish a Royal Commission. The next requirement was to pick a chairman who would increase the chances that its final report would go with the grain of ministerial prejudice. On Wednesday November 5, 1975, Mrs Castle held a private dinner at the Old Russia restaurant for her Health Minister, Dr David Owen, her special advisers, Jack Straw and Professor Brian Abel-Smith, and some of her allies in the public service unions. She takes up the story:

Over drinks before the meal, I had casually raised the question of the chairmanship of the Royal Commission on the Health Service. Had they any suggestions? To my surprise, Audrey [Audrey Prime of NALGO] said enthusiastically, 'Yes, Merrison' [Alec Merrison, then Vice Chancellor of Bristol University]. David and I were rather taken aback, but as she had served with him on the Merrison Committee [the Committee of Inquiry into the regulation of the medical profession, 1973-1975], she was in a better position than any of us to judge his attitudes to the NHS and the things in which we believe [my emphasis]. She was emphatic that he was a dedicated supporter of the NHS and she was sure he would have no truck with private financing and all that nonsense. David and I agreed afterwards that this made Merrison a very serious contender for the job(16).

Alec Merrison duly got the job - and a knighthood. Ten years later, David Owen was quite candid about the episode. In an interview for BBC Radio 3, the following exchange took place:

OWEN: Sadly, politicians have rigged Royal Commissions ... I've been party to that myself, I'm afraid, so I plead guilty.

HENNESSY: Which one did you rig - the Merrison one on the National Health Service?

OWEN: The National Health Service, that's the one, yes. That was rigged basically. I mean it was ensured that [it] was not going to come out with a powerful minority report [which] would oppose the basic principles of the National Health Service ... I would claim it was done for higher motives. But it was rigged(17).

Sir Alec Merrison is a highly regarded scholar and administrator-cum-chairman. It is unfair to infer from Mrs Castle's Diary and Dr Owen's recollection that he was or is an unqualified placeman and a creature of crude political patronage. But other documentary fragments from the postwar private life of the G and G do attest to the kind of amateurism which led Sir Michael Edwardes, in the context admittedly of private companies, to rail against the absence of 'a system for appraising the calibre and performance of people' which, Sir Michael said, switching to the example of government ministers, means that 'nobody tries to measure their intelligence, leadership, drive or any other damn thing'(18). What

15

would Sir Michael have made of this gem from the Cabinet minutes for 1954? The issue is the composition of the new Independent Television Authority, precursor of the Independent Broadcasting Authority, which was to preside over a great engine of commercial and media growth in the 1950s and 1960s. Peopling it was a standard G and G exercise overseen at ministerial level by the Postmaster General, Earl de la Warr. The matter reached Cabinet, the highest decision-taking forum in the land, on July 26, 1954:

> The Postmaster-General said that it was important that the Authority should be appointed and should set to work without delay. Unless it could hold its first meeting before the end of the summer the Authority might not be able to initiate the programmes until towards the end of 1955. The Authority would have an advisory function, and the qualities required in the Chairman and members were tact and sound judgement rather than energy and administrative ability [my emphasis](19).

Matters did not change much over the next 30 years. I remember a permanent secretary exploding over the lunch table in the early 1980s, when speaking of the G and G, 'They are the real amateur element in the system, not us; and they're not even gifted amateurs'(20).

We have seen the high politics and personality of the deployment of the patronage weapon at prime ministerial and ministerial level. Its philosophy, as adumbrated by Earl de la Warr, defies parody. But how are the 'other ranks' found? In the 1950s the Treasury possessed both advantages and disadvantages in fulfilling its head hunting responsibilities. Its operation seems to have been a rather hit and miss affair. Lord Plowden, himself never far from the top three of the G and G in the last 30 years, remembers as head of the Treasury's Central Economic Planning Staff in the early 1950s that 'the list of the great and the good was fairly short. Some of the people on it were dead. No-one knew who to go to. I sent a private memo to Norman Brook saying that an attempt must be made to widen the list and keep it up to date'(21).

Yet Lord Plowden's pedigree illustrates perfectly the rich endowment of human capital the G and G embodied in his generation thanks to Adolf Hitler. As a young businessman he was recruited to the Ministry of Economic Warfare, one of a glittering group of temporary civil servants rushed into Whitehall in 1939-40 to run what turned out to be the most throroughly mobilised of the combatant nations(22). Plowden was one of the most successful of the temporaries. By the end of the war he was at the age of 38 Chief Executive at the Ministry of Aircraft Production. He was recalled to Whitehall in 1947 to run the Attlee Administration's new Central Economic Planning Staff(23). Lord Plowden's G and G record passes through the Chairmanship of the United Kingdom Atomic Energy Authority 1954-59, the Treasury's Committee of Inquiry into the Control of Public Expenditure 1959-61, the Foreign Office's Departmental Committee on the Organisation of Representational Services Overseas, 1963-64, swiftly followed by the Committee on the Future of the Aircraft Industry, 1964-65 and the Standing Advisory Committee on the Pay of the Higher Civil Service 1968-70. In 1986, at the age of 79, he is still active as Chairman of the Top Salaries Review Body which, once a year projects him into the newspaper headlines, as whatever recommendations the TSRB produces for the remuneration of permanent secretaries, judges and generals, the result is invariably one of public and parliamentary outrage. The Plowden family are, in fact, the nearest post-war Britain has come to possessing a Whig dynasty: Lady Plowden is a former Chairwoman of the Independent Broadcasting Authority and has a fistful of influential reports to which her name is attached; son William was once a member of the Central Policy Review Staff and now runs the Royal Institute of Public Administation which, under his leadership, has spawned several important enquiries of its own; son Francis, of Coopers and Lybrand, has been an influential shaper of the Thatcher Administration's financial management initiative as a consultant to the joint Treasury/Management and Personnel Office Financial Management Unit.

Lord Plowden, though a near permanent figure at the elbow of the mighty since 1939, is not the best known of the bearers of British brainpower who were mobilised for total war. That honour falls to J.M. Keynes, as Edward Shils demonstrated in his celebrated essay, 'The Intellectuals and the Powers' when he composed a litany of influential insiders over two millenia:

Equal in antiquity to the role of the highly educated in state administration is the role of the intellectual as personal agent, counsellor, tutor, or friend to the sovereign. Plato's experience in Syracuse, Aristotle's relations with Alexander, Alcuin's with Charlemagne, Hobbes and Charles II prior to the Restoration, Milton and Cromwell, Lord Keynes and the Treasury, and the 'Brains Trust' under President F.D. Roosevelt, represent only a few of the numerous instances in ancient and modern states, oriental and occidental, in which

17

intellectuals have been drawn into the entourage of rulers, their advice and aid sought, and their approval valued(24).

Keynes was sui generis. Summoned to the Treasury by Basil Blackett, his friend from India Office days, on the outbreak of World War 1, he raced from Cambridge on August 2, 1914 in the sidecar of his brother-in-law's motorcycle within days he had solved the currency crisis afflicting the Bank of England; within three weeks he was back at Cambridge working on proofs of A Treatise on Probability(25). So ended perhaps the most dynamic and effective example of the Great and Good as Whitehall's auxiliary fireman. In 1939-40, Keynes along with other veterans from the Kaiser's War, such as William Beveridge, Walter Layton and Arthur Salter(26), had to wait rather longer for Whitehall to acknowledge its need of their intellectual reinforcement. But by the end of the war, Keynes was the key figure in the British team at Bretton Woods, in close and regular touch with Sir John Anderson, the Chancellor of the Exchequer(27). When hostilities had ceased he could not return to the Covent Garden Trust, to his books and the nascent Arts Council of which he was chairman till the American Loan was secured(28). Within four months the accumulated exertion had killed him.

Keynes' last effort on behalf of his country stimulated the couplet which should be emblazoned on the escutcheons of those glistening wartime temporaries. It can be found in the anonymous verse discovered among British papers dealing with the negotiation of the American loan. It reads:

> In Washington Lord Halifax whispered to Lord Keynes,
> It's true they have the money bags, but we have all the brains(29).

In bulk terms, the brainpower mobilised for war by the Ministry of Labour's compilers of the Central Register - a remarkable operation run by Beryl Power which between Munich and the outbreak of hostilities accumulated some 80,000 names kept on cards in a shop in Chiswick High Road(30) - was much younger than Keynes' formidably experienced intellectual equipment. Some of the most successful were complete unknowns in public life before 1939. Sir John Winnifrith, a senior Treasury career official, who as a post war second secretary oversaw the patronage work of his department, said of the wartime generation, 'It's very unlike the Great and Good. They really were winners'(31).

However great Whitehall's failure to replicate in peacetime

its marvellously wide trawl of the capable and the innovative between 1939 and 1945, Miss Power's recruits represented a pool of people on which the post-war G and G was to draw continually. The names of Oliver Franks (Ministry of Supply, 1939-46), Cyril Radcliffe (Ministry of Information, 1939-45) and John Maud (Ministry of Food 1941-44) crop up repeatedly, in Franks' case until the early 1980s. Post-war Whitehall also failed to repeat at in bureaucratic terms the feat of Mr Frank Gent and his team in 569, Chiswick High Road, as Lord Plowden's memo to Sir Norman Brook bore witness. Though to be fair, the wartime list of the Great and Good in the Treasury should not be confused with Beryl Power's Central Register in the Ministry of Labour. They were compiled by different people for different purposes, though, no doubt, some of the names overlapped.

For a large part of the period since 1945, the G and G were managed by Miss Mary Bruce, a Treasury principal who reported direct to successive Heads of the Home Civil Service. Miss Bruce was described by a former colleague as 'a silver-haired diminutive lady with sewn-up lips'. She is remembered as 'an institution, the repository of all knowledge, she would only speak to those who needed to be spoken to. Everyone was terrified of her. It was said that she liked horses more than people. She would come into the office on Saturdays wearing jodhpurs'(32). For Miss Bruce the process of selecting the Great and the Good required absolute secrecy. She dealt very much on a personal basis with her permanent secretary. 'It was all very ad hoc', said one insider, 'names were on different lists - for example there was a national-ised industries list - but it was never brought together'(33). Miss Bruce took over the list in 1950 and died in harness in 1973 at the age of 57.

Some 20 years after Lord Plowden's attempt to stimulate reform, another Whitehall amphibian tried again. Acting on a suggestion from Reginald Maudling, Home Secretary in the Heath Administration, Lord Rothschild, the first head of the Central Policy Review Staff, examined the system. 'I may be wrong', Lord Rothschild recalled, 'but I thought I detected some resistance on the part of the authorities to the Think Tank studying this subject. Patronage is ... a very precious and delicate commodity, and the list of the Great and Good is jealously guarded, no doubt for good if not great reasons'(34). The tank took a look anyway. Its report remains classified. A hint as to its contents can be found in a lecture Lord Rothschild delivered after leaving Whitehall:

PHOTOGRAPH OF MR JONATHAN CHARKHAM

Obviously, the selection of the right people for these critical posts should be hived off ... from the politicans and the Civil Service; and the independent selection panel should not be headed by an emeritus member of either class. But this pipedream won't come true. To paraphrase Clemenceau or Talleyrand, patronage is too serious a matter to be left to outsiders(35).

The initiative was chewed up by the Whitehall machine. 'They did set up a committee', said one insider, 'and that killed it'(36).

After the fall of the Heath Government in 1974, reform of the G and G found another powerfully placed patron in Dr Bernard (now Lord) Donoughue, head of Harold Wilson's new Downing Street Policy Unit who acted without knowledge of the Rothschild initiative:

I had no idea Victor had done that. I was just appalled by the lists that came out of the Civil Service Department [which had taken over responsibility for the G and G in 1968] of people for jobs - the same old names and the same old hacks. So I discussed it with Richard Graham, a member of my unit. He said 'what we need is a little unit whose job is to travel and advertise and actively look for good people.' I drafted a paper to the Prime Minister suggesting a public appointments unit. The PM supported it(37).

Sir Douglas Allen, Head of the Home Civil Service, commissioned an internal review in response to the impetus from No.10. Mr Richard Poland, a retired under secretary from the Department of the Environment, was recalled to the colours to undertake it(38). As a result of the Poland Report, a Public Appointments Unit (PAU) was established in the old Admiralty Building, headquarters of the Civil Service Department. As its founding Director, Sir Douglas Allen chose Jonathan Charkham, a businessman who had come late to the Civil Service as a direct entry principal and who had, by 1975, reached the rank of assistant secretary. Mr Charkham, an immensely personable man, had an open and engaging style. His own version of his job description - 'to find chaps of both sexes for posts'(38) - contrasts vividly with the dry formal remit of the PAU, the latest version of which reads as follows:

(1)   Maintain the Central List [the formal name for the List of the Great and Good] of people who might be considered for full or part time public appointments; pursue

21

all appropriate ways of strengthening the Central List by seeking and receiving advice from all sources including the public representative organisations and government departments.

(2)   Provide advice to departments whose Ministers are responsible for public appointments by suggesting against their specifications names of people from the Central List, or by advising on candidates under consideration who have been recommended to departments from other sources.

(3)   Provide advice to the Head of the Home Civil Service on public appointments (other than Civil Service appointments).

(4)   Co-ordinate, as necessary, policy and information relating to public appointments; advise departments on procedures; and other miscellaneous tasks(40).

On taking over the legendary list, Mr Charkham was told a cautionary tale: 'During the war, in response to suggestions from Mr Churchill for a particular appointment, Lord Halifax minuted "Prime Minister: of the three candidates you suggested I much prefer the two who are dead"'(41). In his seven years as Director of the PAU Mr Charkham always managed to heed that warning - just.

HENNESSY: Did you in your time make any frightful mistakes like serving up a stiff or a member of the criminal classes who got through the net?

CHARKHAM: (Pause) None that we weren't able to retrieve at the eleventh hour'(42).

The list was at a low ebb when Mr Charkham inherited it. A team of six had been engaged on the work in what was very much a backwater on the personnel management side of the Civil Service Department. It consisted of about 3,000 names. The Charkham brief was to find new blood. Some blood groups were at a particular premium - under 40s, women, and people from outside the golden triangle of the South East. He toured the country like a latter-day Wesley preaching the new message about 'chaps of both sexes' to professional and public organisations. Mr Charkham opened the whole process up. He gave interviews to the press. He was photographed leaning against the filing cabinets in which the particulars of the G and G were stored. 'Jonathan Charkham' said a colleague 'demystified the list. It is now a working tool'(43). Bit by bit, the list improved in the desired directions. By 1981 it contained 3,900 names, 16 per cent of whom were women(44).

In one area the momentum of reform broke on the rock of ministerial prejudice. Bernard Donoughue and Richard Graham had wanted both a wider trawl and an advertising programme. Plans were prepared for notices to be placed in Post Offices encouraging people to nominate themselves or their friends for possible inclusion on the Central List. When the idea reached Cabinet committee, it was killed by Labour ministers led by Peter Shore, Secretary of State for the Environment, as Lord Donoughue remembers:

> Whether it was the views of the sponsoring ministers themselves or whether it was their departmental briefing or a mixture of the two, but certainly the sponsoring ministers, especially from the social service and housing and that side, resisted it. I think that they didn't want to give up a piece of power, although in general it was not a power that they had the time or the energy or the knowledge to exercise very well ... I remember Peter Shore very strongly resisting and making the ... totally conservative case for the tried and trusted procedures(45).

It needed a change of government before phase two of the reform could be implemented. In February 1980, when facing questions from the all-party House of Commons Treasury and Civil Service Committee, Mr Charkham was asked if the idea of opening up the public appointments system through advertising had borne fruit. 'Not yet', he replied, 'Nor is it dead'(46). The notion eventually blossomed at the unearthly hour of 6.17 am on the morning of August 5, 1980 during an all-night debate in the House of Commons. Replying to a speech on ministerial patronage from that devoted observer of the G and G, Bruce George, Labour MP for Walsall South, Paul Channon, then Minister of State at the Civil Service Department, told a near-deserted chamber:

> The list is always capable of improvement and expansion, and I would welcome suggestions from the Hon. Gentleman [Mr George] of suitable people to be put on the list. Indeed, I would welcome that from any Hon. Member or from any

member of the public. If they want to suggest the names of people who would be valuable in the public interest, I shall ensure that they are carefully considered(47).

The most dramatic democratic breakthrough in nine centuries of great and gooding went unnoticed for several days until The Times, whose publication had been stopped by a journalists' strike, finally ran a story on August 30(48).

The immediate result of the Channon declaration was that 150 people wrote to Mr Charkham. 'All the applications were serious and were carefully considered', he said later. 'There was no evidence whatever that cranks wrote in. Probably about half went onto the list immediately'(49). By November 1981, a further 450 had written in(50). Following the Channon reform, self-nomination forms were sent to all inquirers (the one in current use is reproduced as Appendix 3). So from the summer of 1980, to the search for more women, more under-40s and more provincials was added something of an open page policy. A great deal had been done in procedural terms to allay criticism of elitism and the closed door, though misunderstandings which created a deeply unfortunate impression could sometimes arise. For example, the Central List does not seek to include trade unionists as trade unionists. Since an agreement between the Wilson Government and the Trades Union Congress in 1968, the Department of Employment has fed in all the names drawn from organised labour, a fact which Mr Colin Peterson, who suceeded Mr Charkham in 1982, took pains to point out(51). Under Mr Peterson, who had previously served in No.10 as Appointments Secretary helping successive prime ministers pick bishops (he was affectionately described as 'heaven's talent scout'(52)), the new system containing the 1975 and 1980 reforms bedded down. In 1984, Mr Peterson left the Civil Service to become Assistant to the Bishop of Winchester. Mr Charkham is now a Chief Adviser at the Bank of England, which led one Cabinet Office wag to remark that 'one has gone to God, the other to Mammon'(53).

The current PAU team in the Cabinet Office Management and Personnel Office consists of Mr Geoffrey Morgan, Director, an under secretary who manages the list in addition to other duties; Mr Geoffrey Wollen, Deputy Director, an assistant seretary who, like his chief, performs his G and G tasks part time; Mr David Barrows, Assistant Director is at principal rank the most senior official in the team devoted whole time to appointments work. Supporting Mr Morgan, Mr Wollen and Mr Barrows are three executive officers and four clerical and secretarial staff. The whole operation costs £146,000 a year(54).

The latest data (January 1986) supplied by the PAU shows that the number of names on the Central List has increased from 3,900 in 1981 to 4,500 in 1983, 4,954 in 1984 to 5,143 now. Its ingredients are as follows:

Cabinet Office

Central List (at 20 January, 1986)

Total number of names - 5,143
Men	4,212
Women	931

Those aged 40 and under - 239 (i.e. born in 1945 or later)
Men	128
Women	111

Geographical distribution
London and South East	2,348	(gross 3,475*)
Rest of the United Kingdom	2,795	

* including those who work in London and the South East but reside elsewhere.

Source: Public Appointments Unit.

The impact of the Channon reform is now strongly visible. Some 20 per cent of those on the current list have nominated themselves, another 10 per cent have been nominated by other outside individuals. A further 20 per cent have been nominated by representative bodies such as professional associations. The remaining 50 per cent have come through the official Whitehall sieve as before(55), though some names arrive on Mr Morgans' desk by more than one route. The PAU remains highly impressed by the quality of people flowing in through the self-nomination channel. Fears that the self-important would dog the system have not been realised. 'English modesty' suggested one insider, 'has proved to be the safeguard. Some self-nominees are interviewed and it has been found in some cases that modesty has caused them to take too narrow a view of their potential'(56).

In addition to the 5,143 names on its active list, the PAU keeps another 15,000 in reserve on its micro-computer, some of whom may be needed to replenish the 40,000 public appointments which need to be filled at any one time. The reservists, for example, consist of the over 65s and categories of people whose skills and experience are already in plentiful supply on the active list. Names on the list are kept confidential. The 238 categories fed in to the PAU computer, to enable it to reply convincingly to a wide combination of individual requirements, are not released either. But the general headings include the sponsoring source, that is, department, professional body or ministerial (the list is not politically segregated, skill and experience rather than prejudice is the criterion for inclusion, though what ministers do with names supplied by the PAU is another matter); language and professonal qualifications; overseas interests, special characteristics, such as an individual belonging to an ethnic minority (though no specific questions are asked here) or taking an interest in the elderly or the treatment of offenders; functional specialisms like industrial relations, farming, management or research and development; most of the computer categories fall under employment characteristics which distinguish between manufacturing and service industries, public service and education, the entertainments industry and the arts, politics and trade unionism. There is a code for job status where applicable and finally the suitablity of an individual is entered on the computer which distinguishes between deliberative function (i.e. committee of enquiry or Royal commission), executive action, (for example, a senior job in a nationalised industry) or an appointment of special responsibility (which can cover a host of one-offs)(57). Those whose names are name is on the list can if they wish, check how they and their particulars are recorded. And these days, all the G and G, the 'great' as well as the merely 'good' are on the computer for the sake of completeness.

The imperatives of the 1975 and 1980 reforms are still felt by the Cabinet Office's talent scouts. The proportion of women on the list continues to increase. It rose from 16 per cent in 1983 to 18.1 per cent by January 1986 (intriguingly, a higher proportion of those actually holding public appointments are women - some 20 per cent of the 40,000). Still more are being sought. Mr Wollen is applying his past experience at the Equal Opportunities Commission and the continuing assistance of the Women's National Council and other professional bodies is being applied to the search. 'Women', said one insider, 'are a reservoir we need to tap'(58). Readers keen to take the initial step into Whitehall's world of patronage should write to:

Mr Geoffrey Morgan,
Director,
Public Appointments Unit,
Cabinet Office,
Whitehall,
LONDON SW1.

It is hugely ironic that just as the reforms of the G and G began to pay off in the size and mix of the list, ministers, and the Prime Minister in particular, should go off the whole idea of Royal commissions and committees of inquiry as an instrument of policy making. But before turning to the freezing out of the great and the good, it is instructive to examine the biographies of three of their grandest figures in the post war period.

Footnotes

(1)   Sampson, Anatomy of Britain Today, p.312.
(2)   Lord Rothschild, Meditations of a Broomstick, Collins, 1977, p.170.
(3)   House of Commons Parliamentary Debates, August 4, 1980, col. 320.
(4)   Mr Schuller made his highly useful remark during a seminar on 'The Demise of the Good and the Great', part of Dr Jim Sharpe's 'Government in Crisis?' series at Nuffield College, Oxford, on November 29, 1985.
(5)   Public Record Office PREM 11/824, Colonial Policy - Immigrants, Brook to the Prime Minister, June 14, 1955.
(6)   PRO CAB CP(55)32. June 11, 1955.
(7)   Ibid.
(8)   For a short profile of Brook see George Mallaby, Each in His Office, Studies of Men in Power, Leo Cooper, 1972, Chapter 2, pp.47-71.
(9)   PRO PREM 11/824. Brook to the Prime Minister, June 14, 1955.
(19) Ibid.
(11) See Peter Hennessy, Cabinet, to be published by Blackwell, July 1986.
(12) See P.J. Madgwick, D. Steeds and L.J. Williams, Britain since 1945, Hutchinson, 1982, pp.321-5.
(13) Private information.
(14) Private information.
(15) Private information.
(16) Barbara Castle, The Castle Diaries 1974-76, Weidenfeld, 1980, p.541.

(17) 'The Good and the Great', BBC Radio 3, February 4, 1985.
(18) Sir Michael Edwardes, 'UK squanders its management talent', Chief Executive, November 1984, pp.10-11.
(19) PRO CAB 128/27. CC(54)53. July 26, 1954, Item 6.
(20) Private information.
(21) Conversation with Lord Plowden, February 10, 1977.
(22) For a general account of the Whitehall irregulars in World War II see Peter Hennessy and Sir Douglas Hague, How Adolf Hitler Reformed Whitehall, Strathclyde Papers on Government and Politics, No.41, 1985.
(23) Bernard Donoughue and G.W. Jones, Herbert Morrison, Portrait of a Politician, Weidenfeld, 1973, pp.405-6.
(24) Edward Shils, The Intellectuals and the Powers and Other Essays, University of Chicago Press, 1972, p.8.
(25) Robert Skidelsky, John Maynard Keynes, Hopes Betrayed 1983-1920, Macmillan, 1983, pp.289-93.
(26) Hennessy and Hague, How Adolf Hitler Reformed Whitehall, p.30.
(27) For an account of Keynes at Bretton Woods see R.F. Harrod, The Life of John Maynard Keynes, Pelican, 1972, Chapter 13.
(28) For an excellent short account of Keynes generally and his wartime service in particular see Roy Jenkins, Nine Men of Power, Hamish Hamilton, 1974, pp.1-26.
(29) Richard N. Gardner, Sterling-Dollar Diplomacy, expanded edition, McGrawHill, 1969, p.xvii.
(30) Hennessy and Hague, How Adolf Hitler Reformed Whitehall, p.19.
(31) Ibid., p.31.
(32) Private information.
(33) Private information.
(34) Lord Rothschild, Random Variables, Collins 1984, p.74.
(35) Rothschild, Mediations of a Broomstick, p.170.
(36) Private information.
(37) Conversation with Dr Bernard Donoghue, 4 July 1984.
(38) Private information.
(39) Private information.
(40) Cabinet Office, Management and Personnel Office, Management Documents 1985-6, available in the MPO Library since August 1985.
(41) Jonathan Charkham, 'Board Structure and Appointments in the Public and Private Sectors', Royal Institute of Public Administration, February 14, 1986.
(42) 'The Good and the Great', BBC Radio 3, 4 February 1985.
(43) Private information.

(44) Figures provided by the Public Appointments Unit.

(45) 'The Good and the Great', BBC Radio 3, 4 February 1985.

(46) Peter Hennessy, 'Whitehall Brief: The Chosen few, Britain, ruled by "permanent coalition" since 1945', The Times, 12 February 1980.

(47) House of Commons Parliamentary Debates, 4 August 1980, col.320.

(48) Peter Hennessy, 'Mr Channon requests more names for the "Great and the good" ', The Times, August 30, 1980.

(49) Peter Hennessy, 'Invitation still open to public', The Times, September 18, 1983.

(50) Peter Hennessy, 'Good and Great list attracts 600', The Times, November 11, 1981.

(51) Peter Hennessy, 'Whitehall Brief: Red letter day for good and great,' The Times, January 18, 1983.

(52) G.W. Jones, 'The Prime Minister's Aides' in Anthony King (editor), The British Prime Minister, second edition, Macmillan, 1985, p.85.

(53) Private information.

(54) Figures supplie by the Public Appointments Unit.

(55) Ibid.

(56) Private information.

(57) Private information.

(58) Private information.

A TRIO OF GRANDEES

That's all right, we can leave it for a day or two to the automatic pilot.
Churchill to Attlee, 1944, on allowing Sir John Anderson to run the country in their absence(1)

Cyril Radcliffe was in the super league. He had everything, intellectual ability, balance, the lot.
Dennis Trevelyan, First Civil Service Commissioner and former secretary of the D-Notice Inquiry, 1986(2)

If Britain became a republic, Oliver Franks would have to be president. No one else would be acceptable.
Former senior civil servant, 1982(3)

To whom at moments of crisis do the powerful in our deferential society defer? The Queen, certainly, and to a handful of eminent figures, highly respected, both high-minded and practical, undeniably above the heat and dust of the political day. The first name that floats across the mind is, by a process of elimination, <u>the</u> number one on the list of the Great and the Good. Not being creatures of fashion or of the cruder kind of political patronage, longevity is a characteristic. In fact, it can be argued that there have been only three since 1945; John Anderson, Viscount Waverley, 1945-52; Viscount Radcliffe, 1952-77, and Lord Franks from 1977 to the present day. All three were Victorians in that they possessed what Ian Bradley has described as 'a call to seriousness'; all three at one time or another were accomplished civil servants and all three were possessed of a presence which made them immensely difficult to gainsay in a committee room; all three were meritocrats in that brain not blood was the substance

PHOTOGRAPH OF LORD WAVERLEY

which accounted for their pre-eminence; and all three would have made superb Viceroys of India.

They are worth singling out for the purposes of this study for a number of reasons: it is intriguing to map the career path which can project a man to the summit of public life while raising him above political taint (our grandees have been indispensable to every post-war premier from Attlee to Thatcher); the personal characteristics and committee room techniques which make up their G and G tool bag are revealing; the assumptions and nostrums that constitute their mind sets even more so; if the G and G is to reach its millennium, where is the successor generation to come from in the absence of Empire and a wartime Civil Service?

The apostle of orderly administration(4)
Lord Waverley, 1882 -1958

There can be no doubt that it is the Prime Minister's duty to advise Your Majesty to send for Sir John Anderson in the event of the Prime Minister and the Foreign Secretary (Sir Anthony Eden) being killed.
Winston Churchill to King George VI, January 28, 1945(5)

When it comes down to serious business there is, I have found, little room for fads and fancies or for those political nostrums that merely make a transient and meretricious appeal.
Sir John Anderson, Election Address to the Scottish Universities, 1938

John Anderson was the complete servant of the state, a man for whom one could feel admiration but never warmth. Whether it be in Dublin Castle during the Troubles, the Home Office during the General Strike, the Governor's residence in Bengal during the riots or the Treasury during the war, he persisted in viewing life from the wrong side of a collar-stud. The pomposity of the address to his electorate in 1938 sprang not only from the aloof manner which dogged him throughout life, but from a genuine conviction, also lifelong, that he was above politics. 'John', wrote his biographer, 'steadfastly refused to recognise that he had in any way descended to the level of election canvassing. This he felt was beneath him; it was a part of that vulgar side of party politics for which he had neither liking or affinity'(7). Though as we shall see, his political opponents did not see it that way - a perception which was eventually to end his No.1 rating on the G and G scale.

If any political figure deserved Nye Bevan's withering description as 'a dessicated calculating machine'(8) it was Anderson.

For he was that rarity among senior civil servants, not to mention politicians, a first class scientist, a chemist and a mathematician, who followed the classic scholarship boy's route from George Watson's to Edinburgh University and a spell of research at Leipzig into the chemical properties of uranium. He was proud of his intellectual equipment, but conscious of the limitations of even the most accomplished intellectual athletes. He once remarked that he did not believe anyone could really concentrate for more than 20 minutes at a time(9).

Anderson trod the meritocratic path into government, taking the Civil Service examination in 1905. He secured the second highest mark ever achieved(10). Appointed to the Colonial Office he promptly penned, for the benefit of his old school, a homily on how to succeed in the competition. Published in The Watsonian, it is stunning in its pomposity and suggests that Anderson never had a youth. How about this for a chatty intro from a 23 year-old to his erstwhile school chums:

> As this joint examination for the three dignified services of the Home Country, the Great Dependancy, and the Crown Colonies is beyond doubt the most severe competitive test in the country, both on account of the scope and variety of the subjects, and from the fact that success in it is a cherished ambition of many of the most earnest students in every one of our universities, a few suggestions from one who has had occasion to give the matter some thought may be of service to young aspirants(11).

For all the gravitas, which led him to be nicknamed Old Jehova, Anderson fitted perfectly the lofty Northcote-Trevelyan ideal of the high-minded, disinterested servant of the state, calm, swift and efficient, which explains Whitehall's tendency to move him from one area of high and/or difficult activity to another. Sir John Bradbury commandeered him from the Colonial Office to join the immensely gifted team of officials constructing the embryonic welfare state with Lloyd George's National Insurance Act, 1911, as their charter(12). By 1920 he was in Dublin Castle and under secretary in the Irish Office, attempting to manage the unmanageable as the Southern Counties endured the successive convulsions which ended British Rule. By January 1922, at the age of 40, he reached permanent secretary rank as Chairman of the Board of Inland Revenue.

Within three months he had moved to the Home Office as its permanent secretary. The man and the institution suited each other to perfection. Jehova had come into his kingdom and he was to stay there for ten years. His was the mind which fashioned the instrument - the Supply and Transport Organisation - that enabled Baldwin to win the General Strike(13). Anderson ran the Home Office almost as a personal fiefdom. Even in Roy Jenkins' time as Home Secretary in the mid-Sixties, the legend lived on. Jenkins, writing of his own permanent secretary, Sir Charles Cunningham, said:

> He was firmly in the tradition of strong, long lasting Home Office permanent secretaries. This tradition dated back at least to Sir John Anderson and probably well before that. It was epitomised by a story relating to Anderson in his heyday. A paper originating with an assistant principal bearing the initials (let us say) of HMT worked its way up to the Secreary of State. The minute from HMT recommended course A. This was not merely opposed but excoriated by everyone else on the way up. The general tenor of the subsequent minutes was that any man in his right mind must clearly accept course B. But not the Secretary of State. He was not one of the more distinguished occupants of this post. But on this occasion he allowed an element of daring to creep through his habitual timidity. 'I think I rather agree with HMT' he somewhat tentatively wrote. The next minute was less tentative: 'I have spoken with the S of S. He no longer agrees with HMT. JA'. Anderson had intervened. The file was closed(14).

In 1932, Whitehall's supreme fireman was drafted to Bengal to douse an incendiary mixture of nationalism and Muslim-Hindu animosity. As Governor, 60 million citizens of the great dependancy, as he had described India in his disquisition in The Watsonian, came under his care, a population nearly 20 million greater than that of the United Kingdom at that time. His biographer describes Anderson's five years in Bengal as 'A record of unqualified and almost unparalleled success'(15), with disorder quelled, bankruptcy averted and the condition of the rural poor improved. Having turned down Neville Chamberlain's offer of the High Commissionership in Palestine he returned home to be made a Privy Counsellor. While on board the P and O liner on the way home, Anderson was invited to let his name go forward as a possible successor to Ramsay MacDonald, who died in November 1937, as MP for the Scottish Universities. After some hesitation he accepted and was elected to Parliament in February 1938. Within eight months he was a Cabinet minister.

Anderson was a brilliant contingency planner. Chamberlain made him Lord Privy Seal in October 1938, one month after Munich, to organise civil defence in case of war. When war came he was promoted and became Home Secretary and Minister for Home Security. Anderson survived Churchill's purge of the 'old gang' in 1940 simply because he had become indispensable. When in 1943 there was talk of his being sent to Delhi as Viceroy, Smuts told Attlee 'Don't let Churchill send Anderson away. Every War Cabinet needs a man to run the machine. Milner did it in the First World war, and Anderson does it in this'(16).

From the autumn of 1940, Anderson had effectively run the Home Front as Lord President of the Council. To all intents and purposes, Churchill, with the Chiefs of Staff and General Sir Hastings Ismay, took care of the war and devolved everything else to the Lord President's Committee which became the Cabinet for home affairs. For all his dryness and lack of social warmth Anderson was an official's dream. For example, the hugely gifted group of economists drawn into the War Cabinet Office's Economic Section in 1939-40 had languished for lack of patrons and customers. Anderson's assumption of the Lord Presidency changed all that. As Lionel Robbins wrote later, 'this was delivery indeed'(17). Thereafter home front Whitehall became an adventure playground for the cream of British social science with Anderson presiding like a benign, practical umpire over their competing schemes.

Unknown to his batteries of economists and statisticians, Anderson assumed in 1941 ministerial responsibility for an awesome corner of Whitehall's war making theme park - that devoted to the development of an atomic bomb. Rarely, if ever, can a minister have possessed exactly the right specialist background for a complicated administrative and technical assignment. As Wheeler-Bennett put it in his ever so slightly eulogistic style, 'John's first love had been science, a field in which he had shown considerable promise as a student. Was there not his brilliant paper on explosives written at Edinburgh University and the remarkable coincidence that he had investigated the radio-activities of uranium while a post-graduate student at the University of Leipzig?'(18). Anderson from the start was part of that 'smallest possible circle of ministers and advisers' privy to the bomb project, wrote Professor Margaret Gowing, its offical historian, and 'only two of them, Sir John Anderson and Lord Cherwell, knew continuously and in detail about the whole business'(19).

Even more remarkable than the conjunction of Anderson's scientific background and his ministerial responsibility for Tube

Alloys, as the bomb programme was codenamed, is the manner in which his pivotal role continued in a G and G capacity after the change of government in 1945 when he was no longer a minister (Anderson had become Chancellor of the Exchequer in 1943 but had kept his atomic brief until Churchill's defeat at the polls). The day Japan surrendered, Attlee's Cabinet committee on atomic energy, known as GEN 75 from its Cabinet Office classification, met and agreed that an Advisory Committee on Atomic Energy should be commissioned. Attlee proposed Anderson as its chairman. It consisted of scientists associated with the bomb and representatives of the Armed Forces and Civil Service. Its terms of reference were twofold: '(a) to investigate the implications of the use of atomic energy and to advise the Government what steps should be taken for its development in this country for military or industrial purposes; (b) to put forward proposals for the international treatment of the subject'(20). As Professor Gowing explained, 'the committee was indeed responsible for making the recommendations which led to the first decisions on the shape of Britain's atomic programme and the attitude to international control'(21).

Anderson, while a member of the Opposition front bench (though he continued to remain an Independent MP outside the Conservative Party) was a key arc in the innermost of inner circles on a project which did not even go before Mr Attlee's full Cabinet(22). This was an influence and a placement without parallel in the history of the Great and the Good before or since. As Professor Gowing put it:

> The position of Sir John Anderson as Chairman was especially important. He returned to an office in the Cabinet Office, enjoyed the services of its secretariat and was a quasi-minister. He was consulted on all important telegrams before they were sent off and on most questions of policy that had to be submitted to the Prime Minister. The High Commission in Canada and the British Ambassador in Washington continued to address telegrams personally to Sir John on atomic matters of special secrecy or importance, and it was Sir John who accompanied the Prime Minister on his atomic energy talks with President Truman in Washington in November 1945(23).

Anderson was not only interested in destructive force. The creative had a like place in his scheme of things. Like most top flight G and G, he diverted part of his administrative energies into artistic channels. In 1946 he succeeded Keynes as Chairman of the Covent Garden Trust and in 1950 he chaired a committee established by the Treasury to examine the export of works of art.

When the Conservatives returned to power in October 1951, Churchill wanted Anderson to become 'Overlord' of his economic ministries - the Treasury, Board of Trade and Ministry of Supply. Anderson declined. The 'Overlord' idea did not accord with his traditional concept of Whitehall organisation in peacetime. And he had acquired a desire to make money and did not relish the prospect of having to relinquish the chairmanship of the Port of London Authority and his several directorships(24). He did, however, accept a peerage and entered the House of Lords as Viscount Waverley. His reluctance to return to government freed him, however, to trigger what in retrospect looks like an explosion of Great and Good activities in the early 1950s.

His pre-eminence at that time produced one of the best G and G stories in its nine century life, even though the tale is apocryphal. The Russians, the story ran, sent a high level delegation to Britain at the height of the cold war. They were conveyed from Tilbury, where they had disembarked, to Westminster by launch and were met at the pier by Lord Waverley, Chairman of the Port of London Authority. An early engagement in their programme was with the Chairman of the United Kingdom Advisory Council on Atomic Energy and, to their mild surprise, they found themselves shaking hands with Lord Waverley. That evening at a reception in Buckingham Palace they just happened to come across one of the Sovereign's most trusted Privy Counsellors, Lord Waverley. The next day having expressed a particular interest in Britain's defences against coastal flooding, they found themselves in East Anglia with Lord Waverley who was busy running an Official Home Office inquiry into this phenomenon following the east coast floods. That night, as a farewell present, the Russians were taken to Covent Garden for a gala performance. There they were met by the Chairman of the Board of the Royal Opera House, Lord Waverley. The exhausted delegation returned to the Soviet Embassy and cabled its report to Moscow: 'Comrade Stalin, Britain is not as we thought a democracy. It is an autocracy run by a man called Waverley'(25).

But at the very apogee of his dignity and his G and G influence, crude politics dealt Anderson a blow which dislodged him from his No.1 position. In November 1951, the chairmanship of the Royal Commission on Taxation of Incomes and Profits fell vacant due to the resignation of Lord Justice Cohen. Anderson, a former

PHOTOGRAPH OF LORD RADCLIFFE

Chancellor of the Exchequer and Chairman of the Board of Inland Revenue with a mind like an adding machine (computers, though in production in Manchester, had yet to infiltrate the popular imagination), was a natural choice to succeed him. Churchill and his Chancellor, R.A. Butler, pressed him to accept. When the appointment was announced in the Commons by Churchill on 26 February 1952 there ensued, to Anderson's horror, an outcry from the Labour benches led by a pair of former Chancellors, the two Hughs - Dalton and Gaitskell. The critical motion they tabled made plain their objections. Anderson's attack on the size and cost of the welfare state and Labour's interventionist economic policies between 1945 and 1951 had left scars. For all his insistence on his independence as a parliamentarian, Labour could not accept him as an impartial figure. 'He was particularly pained', wrote Wheeler-Bennett, 'that these accusations should have been made by men with whom he had worked as a loyal colleague in the National Government of 1940-1945'(26). He wrote to Churchill offering to resign the chairmanship and Churchill, reluctantly, accepted it. 'No event' said his biographer, 'in the otherwise serene and successful post war life of John Anderson caused him such offence and spiritual laceration as this episode'(27). His notion of public service was total. He could never accept he had ever stooped into the minefield of political partisanship. His last publicly known words speak volumes about the man. As he lay dying in St Thomas's Hospital in December 1957, the Order of Merit he was due to receive in the 1958 New Year Honours List was brought forward by a few weeks. On hearing that he was to be honoured personally by the Queen in this fashion, Anderson, overcome with pleasure and gratitude said, 'The Civil Service will be pleased about this'(28). Only Anderson could have thought that, said it and believed it.

The eminent Victorian,
Lord Radcliffe, 1899 - 1977
It is not the easiest thing to argue with people like Lord Radcliffe. It is rather like dealing with God.
Privy Counsellor on the Radcliffe Committee on Ministerial Memoirs, 1976(29)

Education has gone wrong. It paralyses rather than inspires. People have lost the sense of tragedy in life that gives quality to action and thought. A sense of gravity is part of the make-up of society.
Lord Radcliffe, 1976(30)

Lord Radcliffe spoke those words to me at his country home, Hampton Lucy House in Warwickshire, on a freezing January morning in 1976. As a young reporter on The Times I had driven from London to see him to talk about the report on ministerial memoirs he had published five days earlier with the help of a team of privy counsellors commissioned by Harold Wilson to repair the breach in the dyke of Cabinet confidentiality caused by the publication of Volume One of the Crossman Diaries(31). The report had been accepted instantly by the Prime Minister. Wilson must have taken great comfort from a typically Radcliffian paragraph in which the old judge spoke of past ministers of the crown regarding themselves 'as bound by the rule to keep their discussions secret and to respect the confidence that each reposed in the other that this should be so'. Lord Radcliffe went on to remark that few people could have thought such a rule had been obeyed in every instance. There had been breakdowns. 'What matters is that it came to be restated'(32).

It was the first and last time I met Lord Radcliffe. He took over as unoffical number one on the List of the Great and Good when he replaced Lord Justice Cohen as Chairman on the Royal Commission on Taxation of Incomes and Profits in 1952 after the Labour Opposition had, to all intents and purposes, vetoed John Anderson. He remained at number one till his death in 1977, apart from a short interruption after his magisterial denunciation in the House of Lords of Harold Wilson's interpretation of his report on the D Notice Affair in 1967(33). As Hugh Noyes wrote at the time, 'In a 25 minute speech he took apart the Government's case with the artistry of a surgeon and at the end left it scattered about the operating theatre headless and limbless'(34). My first impression of him was a trifle odd. He welcomed me and my photographer colleague, Bill Warhurst, with the words that he and his wife were very glad we had come as it gave them an excuse to put the central heating on. Hampton Lucy House is a big country mansion. But, after all, the Radcliffes had a bit of money. He left £351,082 net(35) and when Lady Radcliffe died in 1982, her estate was valued at £587,639 net(36).

The second impression swiftly brushed notions of eccentricity aside and has remained to this day - of a high-minded, highly intelligent man deeply out of sympathy with his age; and of a singular faculty, a gift with words in which his every sentence was perfectly phrased as if it were a precise, measured judical summing up. He spoke warmly of the Victoria era. 'I have lived through all sorts of denigration of Victorian ideas and achievements', he said. 'I have seen the weight of feeling changing. People are beginning to realise what astounding achievements they were'(37). He drew a distinction between the great nineteenth century Royal commissions and his inquiry into ministerial memoirs. 'This committee was a discussion committee, not a fact-finding committee', he said(38). He talked about running committees, the need not to start out with preconceived ideas. If you had them, your colleagues would be 'less susceptible' to your chairmanship. He spoke highly of the quality of the Civil Service. (He was a bit of a hero to his secretaries, officials such as Robert Armstrong, who worked with him on his Committee of Inquiry into the Monetary and Credit system, 1957-59, Dennis Trevelyan, secretary of the D Notice Inquiry, and Michael Moss, who assisted at his inquiry into ministerial memoirs).

Of all the G and G's output, only those reports bearing the names of Lord Radcliffe and Lord Annan (Chairman of the Home Office Committee on Broadcasting, 1975-1977) bore the unmistakable marks of their personal draftsmanship. In the absence of a written constitution, the thoughts of Lord Radcliffe are something of a surrogate:

> Cabinet secrecy has in reality nothing to do with the making of plots ... Is there anything offensive to enlightened and constitutional ideas of today that such a group, committed to the conduct of the central government, should expect to keep to themselves the details of the process of formulation and that each should be able to rely on the other for the observance of such an understanding?(39).

Whatever the contemporary historian might think of that rather stuffy justification of traditional British secrecy, it is far more elegantly phrased than any of the lifeless paragraphs in Questions of Procedure for Ministers. Lord Radcliffe, in the same document, had something to say about history and historians. 'At some point', he wrote, 'the secrets of one period must become the common learning of another'(40). But 'Government is not to be conducted in the interests of history ... the historian cannot have as of right a smooth highway constructed for him through the intricate plans of public administration and statecraft ... There is no sudden flash of light that illumines the whole landscape: we should be surprised if historians would wish that there were'(41). The Radcliffe guidelines on ministerial memoirs now occupy a section of their own in Questions of Procedure for Ministers, a tome of which the current custodian is his old protege, Sir Robert Armstrong, now Secretary of the Cabinet(41).

41

As I left Hampton Lucy, Lord Radcliffe gave me a copy of his Not in Feather Beds. Its contents gave an indication of the background and interests which moulded his personal marque of statecraft: essays on India (he had never really recovered from his impossible task as the drawer of boundaries between India and Pakistan in 1947 and the bloodshed which ensued); the law; the ancient universities; the arts; Kipling, 'The Dissolving Society'. This last essay illustrated his acute sense of tragedy in a postwar society whose conditions, in one way and another, he had spent long hours dissecting in committee rooms:

> We take so much for granted in modern society and by so doing we impose such heavy strains on our good sense. We steam ahead, carefree navigators as if the conduct of democratic society was an easy art. 'Look, no hands'. It is, on the contrary, the most difficult in the world(43).

It was war service in the Ministry of Information which brought Cyril Radcliffe, a KC with a genuinely brilliant record at the Bar, to the attention of the dispensers of patronage. When the war ended, Sir Edward Bridges, Head of the Civil Service, tried to tempt Radcliffe to stay on as permanent secretary in one or other of the major departments(47). After some thought, he decided to return to the bar. Repeated attempts were made to lure him back into quasi-government service. Attlee asked him to chair the newly created National Coal Board(45). He declined, though duty took him to India as Chairman of the Punjab and Bengal Boundary Commissions. In the Fifties, the demands of being number one on the list left him little time for sitting as a Lord of Appeal - the rollcall is relentless inquiries into tax, recruitment to the secret intelligence service(46), security procedures, the Vassall case, Chairman of the BBC General Advisory Council, Constitutional Commissioner for Cyprus, the Board of Trustees of the British Museum, Chancellor of the University of Warwick. No wonder that by 1955 Norman Brook advised Eden to hold him in reserve for the most complex and intellectually demanding inquiries.

In January 1976, he told me that he retained his intellectual curiosity. He had suffered from ill-health but remained a stocky figure with a large, imposing face and a forceful delivery. 'I do not mean to do anything again' he said. 'I'm nearly 77 and you get out of touch'. Back in The Times office I wrote, 'But few in Whitehall would be surprised if he were summoned once more from the tranquillity of Hampton Lucy. No doubt, like Fu Manchu, we shall hear of him again'(47). I was wrong. He was right. Lord Radcliffe died, inappropriately, on April Fools' Day, 1977.

PHOTOGRAPH OF LORD FRANKS

University man
Lord Franks, 1905
My life is my university
Remark attributed to Lord Franks, 1948(48)

One day the temperature was over 100 and all of us were sweating like horses. I looked at Sir Oliver. He was sweating too, but in a different special way. A drop of moisture formed near his right cheekbone and, simultaneously, another near his left. Then those two drops moved neatly down his face in perfect alignment. 'Can you beat that', I said to myself. 'He even sweats symetrically'.
Remark attributed to a member of the United States delegation at the Marshall Plan negotiations, Paris, 1947(49)

Lord Franks is a monument to the English genius for understatement. It comes out in the most famous Franks story, which dates from his spell as Ambassador in Washington 1948-52. A local radio station had the sharp idea of asking the representatives of the great powers what they would like for Christmas. The resulting broadcast was hilarious. It

> cut into a tape recording of a Parisian voice, pregnant with sincerity: 'Pour Noel, I want peace throughout all the world' . Then we asked the Ambassador of the Soviets what he would like most of all today ...' A dogmatic voice on the tape this time: 'For Chreesmas I want freedom for all the people enslaved by imperialism, wherever they may be'. ... Finally folks, we asked Her Majesty the Queen's Ambassador from London, Sir Oliver Franks, what he would prefer this day ... The diffident tones of Bristol Grammar School and Oxford came on the air: '... Well, as a matter of fact, it's very kind of you, I think I'd quite like a small box of candied fruit'(50).

His shunning of the limelight is genuine. He has consistently given the impression that each time the call to public duty has sounded - from the Ministry of Labour in 1939 with its instruction to 'Go to the Ministry of Supply'(51), from Ernest Bevin in 1947, this time the destination was Paris and the subject the European Recovery Programme(52), and from Clement Attlee in 1948 with a request that he accept the Washington Embassy(53) - he would much rather have stayed in his university. He believes in universities in a way which is immensely unfashionable in the 1980s. But then fashion, intellectual or otherwise, has never bothered Lord Franks. If, as a journalist you pay him a visit in his old farmhouse in North Oxford, he will greet you in a magnificent double-breasted suit straight out of the big band era. Though he is a shy man, he has no qualms in the presence of journalists. He once told me his experience in Washington taught him familiarity with the media. Only once was he non-plussed. It was at the press conference to launch NATO in 1949. A propos of nothing, a lady representing an American women's magazine said 'Sir Oliver, were you breast-fed or bottle-fed?'(54).

Listening to Lord Franks one is constantly reminded of the title of the memoirs of his great friend, Dean Acheson, US Secretary of State in the Truman Administration. Franks has invariably been Present at the Creation(55). He joined the Ministry of Supply when 'if you had an idea of what you wanted to do, there was very little to stop you doing it'(56). Just after the war, as Permanent Secretary to the Ministry of Supply, he motored with the atomic scientist Sir John Cockroft to a disused aerodrome in Berkshire near Harwell. Cockcroft had said his team working on atomic energy needed to be near a university or they would wither on the vine. As Lord Franks told a seminar nearly 40 years later, 'there on the windswept Berkshire Downs, with rainclouds scudding, Cockroft said 'This is where it will be' . And that was the beginning of Harwell(57). We have already encountered him sweating symmetrically at the Marshall Plan negotiations. The reason Attlee and Bevin prised him out of the Provost's Lodge at the Queen's College, Oxford (the provostship being the summit of his ambition) in 1948 was to help secure a more permanent alliance between Europe and North America. He was intimately involved in the negotiations which led to the North Atlantic Treaty in 1949.

There are parallels with the G and G career of Lord Radcliffe. Like Radcliffe, Lord Franks was offered a permanent post at permanent secretary rank after the war and the top job at the National Coal Board. At various stages British Railways, BP and the Atomic Energy Authority had been floated at him: even the legendary White Fish Authority has been deemed a suitable outlet for his talents. And when he returned home from Washington in 1952, the editorship of The Times, the director-generalship of the BBC, a top post in the Treasury and the eventual succession to Bridges were all offered(58). His heart's desire - the Provostship of Queen's - was filled. So he decided to launch out on a completely different career in the City and chaired a clearing bank, Lloyds, from 1954 to 1962. I once asked Lord Franks why he thought there had been so many attempts to turn him into the Pooh Bah of British public life. 'There is a fashion in these things', he said 'and when you are in fashion you get asked to do a lot. I was in fashion for 10 or 12 years'(59).

In the 1950s, part of the fashion was to offer grandees like Lords Franks and Radcliffe the microphone in the shape of the BBC Reith Lectures. Lord Radcliffe's set on 'Power and the State' were still being quoted 30 years later. For example, Sir John Hoskyns, former head of Mrs Thatcher's Downing Street Policy Unit, began his biting attack on the conservatives of the political establishment in 1983 with Lord Radcliffe's observation that 'The British have formed the habit of praising their institutions, which are sometimes inept, and of ignoring the character of their race, which is often superb. In the end they will be in danger of losing their character and being left with their institutions; a result disastrous indeed'(60). Franks does not possess Radcliffe's linguistic firepower. His Reith Lectures on 'Britain and the Tide of World Affairs', delivered in 1954, were a carefully composed but rather conventional tour of the international scene. But, two years before Suez, he did seize the opportunity to bring home the reality that was all too apparent to him at that meeting in Paris in 1947. With Byrnes of the United States on one side of him and Molotov of the USSR on the other (until the Russians walked out and turned their backs on the Marshall Plan), he realised that Britain still had a voice 'but it was a junior voice'(61). His script on the radio seven years later reflected this perception, which, pre-Suez, was not widely shared by his fellow countrymen. Britain's decision-taking since 1945, said Lord Franks, flowed from an accepted principle that:

> Britain is going to continue to be what she has been, a great power. This is something the British people assume and act upon. Once they see that some action or decision is required by this first principle of national policy, they accept it and do not question further. What is noteworthy is the way that we take this for granted ... Yet what we have taken for granted has not been taken for granted abroad. This is one of the things I discovered in the United States ... It was felt by many Americans that a new pattern was emergng in world affairs. It was the age of nations on a continental scale. There were really only two Great Powers - the United States and Russia(62).

Though no longer seated at the high tables of international diplomacy and having deliberately kept out of Whitehall's inner circles and away from highly visible editorships at the BBC and The Times in favour of a less public profession, Lord Franks continued to imbibe the private pleasures of the G and G, chairing the

Committee on Administrative Tribunals and Inquiries 1956-57, the Commission of Inquiry into Oxford University, 1964-66 and the Home Office Departmental Committee on Secton 2 of the Offical Secrets Act which sat in 1971-72. He admits he enjoys the work:

I do enjoy it. I think the first reason is that I have always found myself with very able members of the committees I have been on, with minds as good or better than my own very often bringing expert deep knowledge into it, and trying to match them; trying to keep up with their minds. And trying to bring them into some sort of agreed unity about the way to tackle a problem. It is to me an exciting form of endeavour. I do enjoy that(63).

He was philosophical, too, about which of his endeavours found favour with those in a position to implement his recommendations and which did not:

Let me draw a comparison between the official secrets committee and the committee on tribunals and inquiries. In the second case tribunals and inquiries, a very great deal of what we recommended was acted on very quickly and in the case of the official secrets committee it wasn't acted on at all. Now, I have always thought that in regard to the outcome of any committee's work it depends in part on the quality of what's done, on whether it is in readable English that a layman can understand if he is willing to give some attention. But it is also in a large part - say 50 per cent - a matter of whether public opinion is ready for it at the time.

Now it happened with tribunals and inquiries that public opinion was ready to make changes and therefore our report was favourably received and acted on with speed. In the case of the Official Secrets Act, the opposite was true. Because every government in power is very reluctant to give up any weapon of power(14).

There is a timelessness about Lord Franks when he talks in this vein. He strikes one as a combination of fireman and umpire on whose services virtually all post-war premiers have had to draw. When I first met him at Blackhall Farm in 1977 I scribbled in my notebook: 'Tall, statuesque, austere looking in grey pin striped suit'. Six years later, on another January day, as we chatted about his forthcoming report on the origins of the Falklands War (of which more in the next section), I scrawled 'on very cheerful, chipper, sparkling form'. What one Oxford friend called his 'sphinx-like' qualities(65) became less apparent on successive encounters. The mid- to late-1970s saw Lord Franks sitting with Lord Radcliffe on ministerial memoirs, repairing the breach opened by the Crossman Diaries, with Lords Shackleton and Carr as 'new blood' on the Political Honours Scrutiny Committee filling the metaphorical breach made by Sir Harold Wilson's notorious 'lavender notepaper' Resignation Honours List. His committee touch remained impeccable. I sat beside him for a weekend as rapporteur to chairman at a Ditchley conference on confidentiality and privacy in November 1978. It wasn't a sweaty occasion, but the proceedings were wholly symmetrical. One official, now very highly placed in Whitehall, purred with pleasure at Franks' per-formance. With Lord Radcliffe recently dead, it was quite clear who had become the new number one. The day after the Ditchley conference broke up, Lord Franks travelled to the Civil Service College in Sunningdale where the Official Cabinet Committee on Official Information, GEN 146, masquerading as 'a seminar on open government', was in session. He was in his element, teaching once more and deploying his philisopher's precision: 'Knowledge is power', he told the deputy and under secretaries. 'It is important to recognise that the issue of open government is about power, political power, a shift in power, it's redistribution'(166). He updated for them his 1972 report on official secrecy published before freedom of information had lifted the issue to a newer and more administratively troublesome plateau(67). The Franks solut-ion for the problem of grafting FOI to the British system of Parliamentary and Cabinet government was unveiled: a Commons Select Committee on Open Government to bring pressure on government while avoiding the courts or an information ombuds-man(68). The Green Paper on open government, published on April 30, 1979 in the dying days of the Callaghan government, floated the idea of a select committee to monitor a code of conduct on openness(69). Lord Frank had been heeded once more.

The Anderson-Radcliffe-Franks phenomenon may strike those under the age of 70 as a peculiar way of injecting advice from gifted outsiders into mainstream policy-making. It cannot be seen as a by-product of the 'great man' theory of government. All three were 'great' in the sense of being 'larger gauge people', as one senior civil servant put it(70). But none of them fits Sir Isaiah Berlin's definition of a 'great man':

A great man need not be morally good, or upright, or kind, or sensitive, or delightful, or possess artistic or scientific talent. To call someone a great man is to claim that he has intentionally taken (or perhaps could have taken) a large step, one far beyond the capacities of men, in satisfying, or materially affecting, central human interests(71).

Writing of Chaim Weizmann, whom he does dub a great man, Sir Isaiah says such a person seems capable, almost single-handed, of transforming radically the 'outlook and values of a significant body of human beings'. And the transformation he or she wreaks must be 'antecedently improbable - something unlikely to be brought about by the mere force of events, by the "trends" or "tendencies" already working at the time'(72).

It cannot be said that any of our trio of grandees came into that category. Anderson was involved in managing the Anglo-American venture which produced the first atomic bomb and Radcliffe had to work at great speed on the new boundaries between India and Pakistan which affected the lives of millions. But neither Anderson nor Radcliffe created the events with which their names are associated. And, by its very nature, no Royal commission or committee of inquiry is ever going to be in a position to release forces which transform a society by cutting in a completely uncontrollable way against its grain. Upright, moral and sensitive the best of the G and G may be, but they are not in business to make reformations. They are, or were, no more and no less than top flight permanent secretaries manque (all three, after all, held the rank for a time) with an overlay of wider experience, great presence, natural dignity and considerable gifts at running committees and other committee people. This makes them highly valuable but not great.

Are they, then, the physical embodiments of some kind of consensus, cartographers of the middle way? Not really. Anderson was uncomfortable with the postwar world. Remember it was his outspoken attacks on the extent and cost of the welfare state which, among other things, caused Labour front benchers to attack his appointment to the Royal Commission on Taxation. He was not one of those 'New Jerusalemers' Correlli Barnett excoriates as destroyers of native British industrial enterprise(73). Radcliffe, as his essays and his reverence for the nineteenth century swho, clearly found the pursuits of many postwar men of political power trivial, damaging and distressing. Of the three only Franks, who took the Liberal whip when raised to the peerage in 1962, seems part of the Beveridgite-Keynesian post-war consensus. To be top flight G and G, then, capacity as a mould breaker or sympathy with current political and economic orthodoxies was not de riguer. The ability to shift business and to find a way through administrative thickets was the key - until Mrs Thatcher's time, that is.

Footnotes

(1) C.R. Attlee, As it Happened, 1954, Odhams, p.149.

(2) Conversation with Dennis Trevelyan, January 16, 1986.

(3) Quoted in Peter Hennessy, 'The lord who sits in judgement', The Times, January 17, 1983.

(4) Anderson is described thus by Sir Harold Kent, In on the Act, Memoirs of a Lawmaker, Macmillan, 1979, p.232.

(5) John Wheeler-Bennett, John Anderson, Viscount Waverley, Macmillan, 1962, p.316.

(6) Ibid., p.185.

(7) Ibid., p.187.

(8) According to political folklore, Bevan applied the phrase to his rival, Hugh Gaitskell. Bevan denied this. He said the phrase, delivered in a speech during the 1954 Labour Party Conference in Scarborough, was directed at a 'synthetic figure'. Bevans actual words were 'I know that the right kind of leader for the Labour Party is a dessicated calculating machine who must not in any way permit himself to be swayed by indignation'. See Michael Foot, Aneurin Bevan 1945-60, Davis-Poynter, 1973, pp.450-2.

(10) Wheeler-Bennett, John Anderson, p.17.

(11) Ibid., p.18.

(12) William J. Braithwaite, Lloyd George's Ambulance Wagon, Cedric Chivers, 1970, pp.36, 281, 302.

(13) Keith Jeffery and Peter Hennessy, States of Emergency, British Governments and Strikebreaking since 1919, Routledge 1983, pp.72-4, 111, 120-5.

(14) Roy Jenkins, 'On Being a Minister', Valentine Herman and James E. Alt (editors), Cabinet Studies. A Reader, Macmillan, 1975, p.211.

(15) Wheeler-Bennett, John Anderson, p.172.

(16) Ibid., p.276.

(17) Lord Robbins, Autobioraphy of an Economist, Macmillan, 1971, p.172.

(18) Wheeler-Bennett, John Anderson, p.290.

(19) Margaret Gowing, Independence and Deterrence, Britain and Atomic Energy 1945-1952, Volume 1, Policy Making, Macmillan, 1974, p.5.

(20) Ibid., p.25.
(21) Ibid.
(22) For a discussion of the bomb and collective responsibility see Peter Hennessy, Cabinet, Basil Blackwell (to be published in July 1986), Chapter 4, 'Cabinets and the Bomb'.
(23) Gowing, Independence and Deterrence, Vol. 1, p.25.
(24) Wheeler-Bennett, John Anderson, pp.352-3.
(25) Hennessy, 'The most elevated and distinguished casualties of the Thatcher years', The Listener, February 7, 1985, p.3.
(26) Wheeler-Bennett, John Anderson, p.381.
(27) Ibid., p.384.
(28) Ibid., p.403.
(29) Quoted in Peter Hennessy, 'The eternal fireman who always answers the call to duty', The Times, January 30, 1976.
(30) Conversation with Lord Radcliffe, January 27, 1976.
(31) Report of the Committee of Privy Counsellors on Ministerial Memoirs, Cmnd 6386, HMSO, January 22, 1976.
(32) Ibid., p.22.
(34) Hugh Noyes, 'D Notices White Paper Savaged, Scathing Attack by Lord Radcliffe', The Times, 7 July 1967.
(35) Latest wills, The Times, 17 June 1977.
(36) Latest wills, The Sunday Telegraph, 8 August, 1982.
(37) Hennessy, 'The eternal fireman', The Times, 30 January 1986.
(38) Conversation with Lord Radcliffe, January 27, 1976.
(39) Report of the Committee of Privy Counsellors on Ministerial Memoirs, p.13.
(40) Ibid., p.29.
(41) Ibid., p.31.
(42) Private information.
(43) 'The Dissolving Society' was the title of Lord Radcliffe's Annual Oration at the London School of Economics, 10 December 1965. It is reproduced in Not in Feather Beds, pp.229-46.
(44) Private information.
(45) Private information.
(46) Private information.
(47) Hennessy, 'The eternal fireman', The Times, 30 January 1976.
(48) 'Highest brow in Whitehall', Daily Mail, 16 February 1948.
(49) Quoted in Paul Bareau, 'Sir Oliver just Keeps Climbing', News Chronicle, 1 November 1954.
(50) Geoffrey Moorhouse, The Diplomats, The Foreign Office Today, Cape, 1977, pp.251-2.
(51) Hennessy and Hague, How Adolf Hitler Reformed Whitehall, p.26.

(52) Hennessy, 'Lord who sits in judgement', The Times, 17 January 1983.
(53) Ibid.
(54) Conversation with Lord Franks, 11 January 1983.
(55) Dean Acheson, Present at the Creation, My Years in the State Department, Hamish Hamilton, 1970.
(56) Hennessy and Hague, How Adolf Hitler Reformed Whitehall, p.36.
(57) Lord Franks at a seminar on his Washington Embassy, London University Institute of Historical Research, 12 October 1983.
(58) Private information.
(59) Conversation with Lord Franks, 24 January 1977.
(60) Sir John Hoskyns, 'Conservatism is not enough', Institute of Directors Annual Lecture, 28 September 1983.
(61) Conversation with Lord Franks, 24 January 1977.
(62) 'Basis of Britain's Greatness, Partnership Replaces Isolation', The Times, 8 November 1954.
(53) 'The Good and the Great', BBC Radio 3, 4 February 1985.
(64) Ibid.
(65) Private information.
(66) Civil Service College, CSC Working Paper No.,5, January 1979, p.1.
(67) Report of the Departmental Committee on Section 2 of the Official Secrets Act, 1911, Cmnd 5014, HMSO, September 1972.
(68) CSC Working Paper No.5, p.9.
(69) Open Government, Cmnd 7250, HMSO, April 1979.
(70) Private information.
(71) Isaiah Berlin, Personal Impressions, Oxford University Press, 1982, p.32.
(72) Ibid., p.33.
(73) Correlli Barnett, The Audit of War, The Illusion and Reality of Britian as a Great Nation, Macmillan, 1986. Chapter One, 'The Dream of the New Jerusalem', is devoted to this theme.

Heath consciously reacted against the Wilson style of buying the hours with beer and sandwiches at No.10, and the years with royal commissions.
Phillip Whitehead, 1985(1)

Probably what she [Mrs Thatcher] objects to about the classical Good and Great is that by their very nature - by the fact that they all know each other, they are 'clubby' people, they frequent the same environment - they do tend to reach moderately balanced medium conclusions about whatever matter they are dealing with.
Sir Anthony Parsons, 1985(2)

When ruling classes are on the run, their womenfolk wear the trousers.
Professor Norman Stone, 1984(3)

Criticism of the Great and Good and their venerable artefacts, the Royal commission and the committee of inquiry, did not wait upon the arrival in No.10 of the most anti-establishment Prime Minister of recent times. Virtually every scholarly examination of offical inquiries contains the obligatory quote from A.P. Herbert, usually an extract from his delightful poem, 'Sad Fate of a Royal Commission', published just fifty years ago:

> I saw an old man in the Park;
> I asked the old man why
> He watched the couples after dark;
> He made his strange reply:
>
> I am the Royal Commission on Kissing

Appointed by Gladstone in '74;
The rest of my colleagues are buried or missing;
Our minutes were lost in the last Great War.
But still I'm a Royal Commission.
My task I intend to see through,
Though I know, as an old politician,
Not a thing will be done if I do(4).

A glance at the list of Royal commissions since 1945 shows none of the 37 to be quite in the kissing category but the 1946 Royal Commission on Awards to Inventors (which took a decade to report)(5) and the 1951 Royal Commission on University Education in Dundee(6) look, as subjects go, a trifle peripheral for such grand treatment. And, in the last year of his premiership, Sir Winston Churchill circulated a note to the Cabinet urging a more sparing use of the device. Sir Ernest Gowers' Royal Commission on Capital Punishment, Sir Winston wrote, 'occupied four and a half years and cost £23,000. It seems to me that the latter figure should be borne in mind when other proposals for Royal Commissions are presented to us'.

Sir Winston's injunction had but a minor impact. Taking simply Royal commissions and not the vastly more plentiful committees of inquiry, six were set up during the six and a quarter years of Labour rule after 1945 - Awards to Inventors (1946); Justices of the Peace (1946); the Press (1947); Lotteries, Gaming and Betting (1949); Capital Punishment (1949); and University Education in Dundee (1951). Twelve Royal Commissions were established during the 13 years of Conservative government which ensued - Taxation of Profits and Income (1951); Marriage and Divorce (1951); Scottish Affairs (1952); the Civil Service (1953); the Law Relating to Mental Illness and Mental Deficiency (1954); Common Land (1955); Doctors and Dentists Remuneration (1957); Local Government in the Greater London area (1957); the Police (1960); the Press (again) (1961); National Incomes (1962) and the Penal system (1964). Harold Wilson turned Royal Commissions into a growth industry. Extract Lord Pearson's Royal Commission on Civil Liability and Compensation for Personal Injury (1973), founded during the Heath interlude, and Wilson's creations accumulate remorselessly: Reform of the Trade Unions and Employers' Associations (1965); Medical Education (1965); Prices and Incomes (1965); Local Government in England (1966); Tribunals of Enquiry (Evidence) Act, 1921 (1966); Assizes and Quarter Sessions (1966); Industrial Relations (1969); Environmental Pollution (1970); the Press (the third time since the war); Standards of Conduct in Public

Life (1974); National Health Service (1976); Gambling (1976) and Legal Services (1976). James Callaghan established one, the Royal Commission on Criminal Procedure (1978). Mrs Thatcher has created precisely none, though the Royal Commission on Environmental Pollution is a permanent body and continues to produce reports(8).

For the waxing and waning of post-war Royal Commissions and departmental committees, the figures are bulkier ,(see Appendix Two on new starts 1945-85), tell a slightly different story and give a more complete picture. Mrs Thatcher has had resort to the departmental inquiry and the committee of privy counsellors but, before treating the Thatcherian onslaught on the G and G, the impact of Wilson must be assessed. For by debasing the coinage through an inflation of commissions, Wilson induced a reaction not only from the prime ministers who succeeded him but from the G and G themselves. They tired of sitting to no purpose.

Lord Rothschild began the revolt of the grandees a fortnight before the report of his Royal Commission on Gambling landed on the Home Secretary's desk. Addressing the annual dinner of the British Academy at the Middle Temple on 29 June 1978(9), Lord Rothschild questioned the utility of such exercises. After quoting A.P. Herbert - 'a Royal Commission is generally appointed, not so much for digging up the truth, as for digging it in' - he asked 'can a system which relies on the goodwill, the evening and the weekends of hard-pressed people be viable in the Seventies and after?'. He tilted at the compilers of the List of the Great and the Good and the Home Office who, between them, had come up with his commissioners:

> None of the members of the Royal Commission on Gambling is a hardened or experienced gambler (indeed few of us indulge in it at all), and there seems to be no particular reason why a philosopher, a sports commentator, a specialist in office organisation, an ex-scientist, an Olympic medallist, a trade unionist, a journalist and two practising barristers should be any better qualified to pronounce on the particular subject than any nine members of the Cabinet; except that the latter are known not to have time, whereas the former are assumed, for some obscure reason, to have the time, the energy and the capacity to learn an entirely new subject and become expert on it(10).

He found it difficult to understand why the Home Office had set him and his commission in operation as its own research unit had undertaken its own review of gambling literature and 'while our Royal Commission was labouring - and parturition has occasioned much labour - a Select Committee of the House of Commons made an investigation in depth into one important aspect of gambling, the Tote, which for obvious reasons, we were also studying. Is there not something incomprehensible about such prodigality, such overkill?'(11). Within a year the fountains of patronage in No.10 were firmly turned down, if not off, by a lady who substituted rationing and parsimony for prodigality and overkill.

By the late 1970s, when Lord Rothschild uttered his lament before the British Academy (not all of whom appeared to relish it(12), presumably because a high proportion of the decorations which enlivened their evening dress had come from national service in the ranks of the Queen's own G and G), fairly savage strictures could be heard in Whitehall against the Royal commission and the committee of inquiry as an aid to policy-making. Lord Donoughue, Senior Policy Adviser in No.10, Downing Street under Wilson and Callaghan, who took the initiative which led to the 1975 reforms, made his reservations public in an interview for Radio 3's 'The Good and the Great'. 'Establishment culture', he said, 'is the culture of sound and comfortable men'. Of those members of the Establishment who are recruited into the G and G he added:

> Their trouble is that they go too far. They never take risks and they never introduce any imagination. So, in the end, you get the situation we have had in which virtually none of the commissions of enquiry ... come up with anything interesting at all and that's why they've become redundant(12).

Dr David Owen, Foreign Secretary in the Callaghan Administration, is a long time Establishment hater. 'I loathe the Establishment', he told Terry Coleman in 1984, 'and always have done. They've never been able to envelop me'(13). The G and G can expect no restoration if an Alliance government is formed with Dr Owen at its head:

> Labour governments, Conservative governments, they all come and go. They [the Establishment] are absolutely secure. They are the ones who were sent out to George or to settle up with Harry ...
>
> If they had to be characterised by anything it is you split the difference on every issue. A certain cynicism ... You never really feel they actually stand for anything. They are just

56

part of the general British slide and decline and they have been a big contributor to it. They are the people who always can find an argument against doing anything, a brilliant analysis as to why you should do nothing. They are the inertial force within the bureaucrcacy and within British life(14).

Even when any personal animosity has been siphoned from the Donoughue or Owen broadsides, the contrast between the wartime temporary Civil Service and the post-war G and G is very marked, amazingly so when, in so many instances, one is talking about the same people. Why did the recruiters to the List of the Great and the Good post-1945 fail to match Beryl Power's performance in 1938-39?

Two reasons are self evident. Munich and the sense of national urgency it created allowed the Ministry of Labour's headhunters to suck up talent, like some giant vacuum cleaner, wherever it was concealed in the British Isles. 'The remotest laboratory, the most obscure department of classics or philosophy were not immune from their attentions'(15). Secondly, the posts the wartime irregulars filled were essentially practical jobs with direct, executive responsiblities - running a division of the Ministry of Supply in the case of Douglas Jay(16), creating a utility furniture scheme in the case of Gordon Russell(17) or designing a more bearable form of rationing with a points system in the case of that formidable collection of brainpower in the Economic section of the War Cabinet Office(18). The post-war G and G were deployed almost exclusively on advisory tasks, not executive. However apt or timely their reports, their recommendations had to grind through the Whitehall mill of inter-departmental working parties and Cabinet committees and to endure that peculiar blend of prejudice, hunch and political calculation of which policy-making so often consists at ministerial level. Even where a Royal commission or committee of inquiry consisted of experience in depth with a proven graduate of Miss Power's academy at its head, its product could appear utterly ineffectual, whatever its intrinsic merits, as adoption and implementation lay in entirely different hands.

This phenomenon, which Bernard Williams immortalised as 'pathways to the pigeonhole', was what fuelled the revolt of the G and G themselves. Professor Williams, a member of the Royal Commission on Gambling (Bernard Williams was the philosopher Lord Rothschild referred to in his address to the British Academy) and chairman of the Home Office's Committee on Obscenity and

Film Censorship, delivered his Grand Remonstrance at the Royal Institute of Public Administration's conference on public influence and public policy at Sussex University in April 1981(19). Commissions and committees, said the Provost of King's College, Cambridge, 'characteristically involve a great deal of work for unpaid participants, and that ... work often seems to be wasted'. He then swung into line with A.P. Herbert:

> This is not simply the point that a report very often fails to lead to any legislation. More than that, the appointment of such a committee seems often designed not to lead to legislation, and to be diversionary. Moreover, although there are ways in which a report can be useful and indeed influence opinion even though it does not lead to legislation, the system is largely designed to prevent those further effects coming about(20).

Professor Williams offered a remedy. No government can be committed in advance to accepting the recommendations of a committee. Its report 'may be divided, or idiotic'. And the government may have changed while it was sitting. 'But any administration should be committed to saying why it does not accept the recommendations, if it does not, and if it is the same administration, it should be institutionally required to show that the committee was set up in good faith, namely out of interest in its answer, and not merely as a way of removing the question'(21). One way to do this, he added, would be to oblige a government to make a reasoned response to the report in a publication and a debate in the House of Commons.

Two years later a similar line was taken by two of the last Royal Commission chairmen the country has seen, Lords Rothschild and Benson. In his British Academy Lecture, Lord Rothschild noted that the last time Royal commissions themselves had been inquired into was 'as recently as 1910'(22). He was referring to the Home Office's Departmental Committee on the Procedure of Royal Commissions on 1909-1910 which sat under the chairmanship of Lord Balfour(23). Lords Rothschild and Benson, while making it plain that the person who should be updating the work of the Balfour Committee was Sir Robert Armstrong, the Secretary of the Cabinet, not them, proceeded nonetheless to do an inquiry of their own which they presented in the form of an obituary and called it 'Royal Commissions: A Memorial'(24).

Royal commissions, said their lordships, now cost in excess of £1m (remember the £23,000 for the Royal Commission on Capital

58

Punishment mentioned by Churchill). They laid down four conditions that should be met before a commission was established: The problem to be tackled must be significant but not urgent as Royal commissions took time; Whitehall did not already possess sufficient information to put before ministers; the evidence needed could only be gathered by research or interviewing a significant number of informed people; when a Royal commission was established it should be stated publicly that there was an intention to act when its report was published(25). They lingered on the importance of picking the right people as commissioners. They had to possess wide general experience, average or above average intelligence, integrity, grasp, a determination to reach a balanced judgement and a moderate political outlook. They must not have intense political or doctrinaire views, prior commitment to a stated view or the views of an organisation or pressure group(26). Lords Benson and Rothschild warned of the perils of second rate minds being let loose on serious matters of public policy:

> Many commissioners, particularly if they are of second quality, start their work in the belief that they will not be doing their job unless they recommend radical changes ... They should be disabused of this idea ... A wise commissioner is the person who only recommends a change when one is clearly needed and when he is satisfied that the new organisation will be better than the one which now exists, particularly if the latter is repaired or strengthened(27).

Finally, in the manner of one of Lord Rothschild's celebrated CPRS reports, they displayed a set of terse conclusions that fitted neatly on one side of A4:

(1) A review of Royal commissions appointed in the last 20 years should be made in order to prevent a waste of public monies in the future.

(2) The quality of commissioners appointed is crucial to success ...

(3) The number of commissionsers should be small and should not exceed ten. The chairman should be consulted before appointments are made.

(4) Guidelines for the use of prospective commissioners should be made ... commissioners should undertake to give up the necessary time before being appointed.

(5) A nucleus of experienced staff of a sufficiently high grade should be appointed to the secretariat. The present ad hoc appointments are not satisfactory(28).

Shortly after the Rothschild-Benson obituary was published the RIPA held a wake in a basement room, just across the road from the Treasury on 15 December, 1982(29). The occasion left a deep imprint on me. It was dominated by the Williams-Rothschild-Benson theses. There was talk of 'the deafening silence syndrome'. I described the seminar as 'a collective whinge' and its participants as 'The Lost Tribe of British Public Life'(30).

For the men and women in that basement room, loaded with honours and dripping with gravitas, knew that since 1979 they had been pretty well frozen out, that talk of reforming the committee/commission system was largely irrelevant for the forseeable future. Mrs Thatcher, on this issue at least, breathed as one with Dr Donoughue and Dr Owen. Clive Priestley, who, as Lord Rayner's chief-of-staff in the Prime Minister's Efficiency Unit, worked closely with her, said Mrs Thatcher 'does have a particular view of the sorts of people who can help her on the missions which she regards as important. Broadly speaking, but not exclusively, she is against the "golden oldie" type, and, I dare say, that would tend to cut out quite a number on the List of the Great and the Good'(31). The Rayner Unit was an example of her preferred method of operating. Mrs Thatcher had no wish to commission a variation of the Fulton Committee on the Civil Service of 1966-68, a prejudice which, as Clive Priestley recalls, Lord Rayner shared:

> Derek Rayner had a strong personal contempt for what he called 'stifling committees', his substitute for the phrase 'steering committee'. He had a very strong commitment to the idea that people of capacity, whatever organisation they served in, can very quickly get to the roots of a problem and make proper, sensible recommendations if properly supported. He was quite clear that if he went for a committee structure or, indeed, a large bureaucracy of his own, he would be very quickly bogged down(32).

But even an anti-G and G premier like Mrs Thatcher has to empanel some committees of inquiry and appoint, whether she likes it or not, a small army to the boards of quangoland. And it is in this latter sector of patronage that she has aroused the fiercest criticism.

The Thatcher effect in this area is difficult to document (as it is in the field of senior promotions in the Civil Service). There is a feeling abroad that 'conviction politics' as practised by a Prime Minister with powerful tempermental likes and dislikes has, to put it no higher, altered conventional procedure, though, as we have seen, 'rigging' went on in the 1970s as Mrs Castle's Diary and Dr Owen's recollections bear witness in the case of the Royal Commission on the National Health Service. But for scholarly purposes, hearsay and supposition are no substitute for documents. Unless or until an equivalent to the Castle Diaries for 1979-86 is published, or a senior figure, whether politician or civil servant, who had participated in the patronage business comes clean in public about this or that appointment, a drizzle of complaint from traditionalists and some prima facie evidence is all we have to work with.

The prima facie material is fairly plentiful. The most convincing comes from Ronald Butt of The Times, a supporter of Mrs Thatcher, who revels in the offence she has caused in the ranks of 'the great and the good among political commentators - whose idea of political neutrality resembles the collected words and deeds of Mr Roy Jenkins and Mrs Shirley Williams'(33). Mr Butt's fire was aroused by the snobbery he detected behind much of the fashionable hostility to the Prime Minister:

> There was the intellectual snobbery which resented her non-acceptance of an establishment which had become unused to challenge. There is a strong whiff of class snobbery. You might think this absurd since Grantham and Somerville is no worse than a mining valley and Balliol. But it all depends on willingness to join the establishment which Mrs Thatcher had the effrontery to challenge with some of the common sense of the suburbs(34).

And it is the BBC which, according to Henry Fairlie in 1959 was 'of all the voices of the Establishment, the most powerful'(35), which now has in Mr Stuart Young, a Thatcher appointee brimming with the common sense of the North London suburbs (Woodhouse Grammar School, North Finchley), that has brought the criticism of current prime ministerial patronage to the fore. Another Times columnist, David Watt, former Director of the Royal Institute of International Affairs and an unashamed defender of 'some of the virtues of the old paternalism'(36) claims that:

> By far the most influential group ... [of the BBC's enemies] ... is made up of those who have a visceral objection to the BBC as the perfect embodiment of the old establishment, the paternalist expression of traditional middle-of-the-road consensus. Thatcherism and the Prime Minister herself, being in

iconoclastic reaction against just these things, are naturally hostile to the BBC; they have also helped to create a polarised political and cultural climate in which Reithian aspirations find it hard to survive(37).

But it was the decision of the BBC Board of Governors, after pressure from the Home Secretary, to ban the showing of the Real Lives television documentary on political extremism in Northern Ireland which led in the summer of 1985 to the more perfervid accusations about supine placemen in the BBC hierarchy. A somewhat bizarre spin-off from this was the paean of praise to the old establishment which poured forth from the pen of the Observer's leader writer:

> ... to blame Mr Young exclusively for the quite unnecessary shambles the Governors have created would be unfair. He had, after all, to work with the material at his disposal; and the days have long since departed when the BBC's Board comprised people of the independence and calibre of, say, Lady Violet Bonham Carter, Sir Harold Nicolson or the redoubtable ... Baroness Wootton(38).

Even an outspoken critic of the G and G like Lord Donoughue maintains that a regrettable precedent has been set by the pattern of patronage since 1979:

> When I was in Downing Street, both prime ministers [Wilson and Callaghan] would make sure that able people from the Conservative side were utilised in public appointments. I think what's very wrong and worrying is the way the present government has made appointments on the basis of only people who agreed with them politically. That is not only bad because the advice is not very valuable; but it's also a very bad precedent for the future ... If you got in a left wing government, they could put up just as many people. I think Mrs Thatcher might come to rue the consequences of that precedent(39).

It is hard to see how the Good and the Great idea can run unless it is lubricated by a cross-party, if not an above-party, philosophy. Clive Priestley believes that it could become difficult to persuade people that a period of public service is time well spent because of 'a very unfortunate and damaging polarity of political opinion and activity in the country at the moment. I think the public generally feels itself demeaned by this and let down by it'(40).

Richard Hoggart has made the running among of those who believe 'the two Thatcher Governments have steadily undermined one of our more useful democratic devices', which he describes as 'arms-length or buffer committees'(41). He shares with Professor Ralf Dahrendorf (a German citizen who, while Director of the London School of Economics, sat on Lord Wilson's inquiry into the City and Lord Benson's Royal Commission on Legal Services) the view that such bodies, in the way they are peopled as well as the way they operate, are a peculiarly British phenomenon. 'Few foreigners understand them', wrote Hoggart, 'or if they understand the words used, can take them at face value. The idea of a committee set up and funded by government which contains members from right across the political spectrum and is ostensibly free to report as it wishes must be a trick, one of Old Albion's characteristically humbug-based forms, a type of repressive tolerance which will in the end not seriously disturb any government or will do so at the peril of its own life'(42).

Hoggart, who suffered what he called a 'manipulated departure' from the vice-chairmanship of the Arts Council - 'it was a political decision, a response to what was felt to be the wish of "No.10" '(43) - was undoubtedly reflecting accurately the tendency to read the PM's mind in the higher reaches of Whitehall departments where patronage decisions are processed. In one non-defence department, for example, there was some nervousness about a particular chairmanship going in the early 1980s to a highly qualified individual because he had spoken against the cost of the Trident missile programme, an issue which had absolutely nothing to do with the post for which he was eventually picked(44). Richard Hoggart added his torch to the searchlight on the BBC Board of Governors - 'Never before has ... [it] ... had both a Conservative chairman [Stuart Young] and a Conservative Vice-Chairman [Sir William Rees-Mogg, who also chairs the Arts Council]'(45). And he rounded off his tirade in defence of the G and G and the arms-length principle by saying that under Mrs Thatcher 'the process is a reflection of the Prime Ministers unshakeable faith in the individualised, centripetal, one-of-us system of government. Against such operations, the old-style quangos, weaknesses and all, shine like a Christmas candle in an imperfect world'(46).

But one has to treat the widely purveyed image of Mrs Thacher as Queen Boadicea driving a chariot of conviction politics through traditional conventions and institutions with a degree of scepticism. To take it at face value, it suggests that the majority of permanent secretaries appointed since 1979 share the values of

63

the Grantham corner shop and believe the Beveridgite-Keynesian consensus to have brought Britain to the brink of disaster. In all probablility, the Prime Minister, even if those were her criteria of preferment, would find it hard to muster a single true believer from the top three grades of the Civil Service. The same applies to Cabinet government. It has not been put on a shelf in the No.10 Registry along with decaying volumes of Sir Ivor Jennings and the late John Mackintosh(47). The same applies to patronage. The BBC Board of Governors may have appeared to be the Government's catspaw when the Real Lives affair began. But a sensible and widely acceptable solution was found in a matter of weeks which projected the programme on to the screen. But take that other grouping crucial to the future of British public broadcasting, the Peacock Committee. True its remit - to examine alternative ways of financing the BBC including advertising - would not have been laid down by any previous government, Labour or Conservative. But the Peacock Committee is not packed by people the Prime Minister would deem 'one of us'(48). Alastair Hetherington is a former editor of The Guardian and ran BBC Scotland before taking up a chair at Stirling University. Mr Sam Brittan, Economics Editor of The Financial Times, may be the brother of Leon, the former Home Secretary who commissioned Peacock, but he is one of the most independent-minded people in British journalism(49). Mr Jeremy Hardie is an SDP candidate. At a push it could be suggested that Professor Peacock, Miss Judith Chalmers, the television personality, Sir Peter Reynolds of Rank, Hovis McDougall and Lord Quinton of Trinity College, Oxford, cut with the Thatcherite grain but there would be inaccuracy and injustice in such a remark.

The most convincing evidence that the G and G, as they approached their nine hundredth anniversary, were down but far from out came in the mopping-up operation after the greatest single crisis of Mrs Thatcher's premierships, the Falklands War of 1982. She promised the Commons an inquiry into its origins. Before appointing a chairman to lead a team of Privy Counsellors, the Prime Minister had to consult the Leaders of the Opposition parties. At such moments all roads lead to North Oxford and Lord Franks. It was clearly a job for the No.1 on the list. Sir Robert Armstrong, Secretary of the Cabinet and a long-time admirer of Franks the man and the Franks style, called at Blackhall Farm one Saturday morning to check that Attlee and Bevin's favourite fireman was able and willing to travel on the G and G flyer from Oxford to Paddington once more. Lord Franks was willing and his committee after, as Mr Callaghan later put it in the Commons, painting 'a splendid picture' in the first 338 paragraphs of their report, behaved in paragraph 339, the last one, as if Lord Franks had 'got fed up with the canvas he was painting and ... chucked a bucket of whitewash over it'(50), a charge Lord Franks firmly denied(51). Whatever the justice of the former prime minister's complaint, the Franks report on the origins of the Falklands War effectively laid the matter to rest in the approach to the 1983 general election. Lord Franks was and remains the safest pair of hands at Whitehall's disposal.

Footnotes
(1)   Phillip Whitehead, The Writing on the Wall, Michael Joseph, 1985 p.54.
(2)   'The Good and the Great', BBC Radio 3, 4 February 1985.
(3)   Norman Stone, 'Margot and the ruling class', The Sunday Times, June 10, 1984.
(4)   This gem first appeared in A.P. Herbert, Mild and Bitter, Methuen, 1936. Herbert's last squib on the subject, which reproduced it, was Anything but Action? Hobart Paper 5, Institute of Economic Affairs/Barrie and Rockliff, 1960, p.6. There was quite a spate of publications on the Royal commission-committee of inquiry theme, the most useful general guide is probably T.J. Cartwright, Royal Commissions and Departmental Committes in Britain, Hodder, 1975. Also valuable are Advisory Committees in British Government, a PEP report, Allen and Unwin 1960; Gerald Rhodes, Committees of Inquiry, Allen and Unwin, 1975; Richard Chapman (editor), The Role of Commissions in Policy Making, Allen & Unwin 1973; and Martin Bulmer, (editor), Social Research and Royal Commissions, Allen and Unwin, 1980.
(5)   Letter from Mr Leon Brittan to Mr Tim Eggar, MP, January 25, 1985, available in the House of Commons Library.
(6)   Mr George Younger, written Parliamentary Answer No. 65, April 16, 1985 in reply to a question from Mr Tim Eggar, MP.
(7)   Public Record Office, CAB 129/70 C(54)264, 'Royal Commissions. Note by the Prime Minister', 4 August 1954.
(8)   For the complete list of post-war Royal commissions see Leon Brittan's letter to Tim Eggar of January 25, 1985 and George Younger's written answer of April 16, 1985.
(9)   Peter Hennessy (a Staff Reporter), 'Royal Commissions' value questioned by Lord Rothschild', The Times, 30 June 1978.
(10) Ibid. The full text of 'Royal Commissions' is reproduced in Lord Rothschild', Random Variables, Collins, 1984, pp.85-91.

(11) Ibid., p.86.
(12) Conversation with Bernard Donoughue, 29 November 1984.
(13) 'The Terry Coleman Interview', The Guardian, 8 September 1984.
(14) 'The Good and the Great', BBC Radio 3, 4 February 1985.
(15) Hennessy and Hague, How Adolf Hitler Reformed Whitehall, p.50.
(16) See Douglas Jay, Change and Fortune, a Political Record, Hutchinson, 1980, p.80.ff.
(17) See CC41. Utility Furniture and Fashion 1941-1951 , ILEA 1974, pp.25-6.
(18) Hennessy and Hague, How Adolf Hitler Reformed Whitehall, pp.40-1.
(19) Peter Hennessy 'Some inquiry committees "meant to achieve nothing" ', The Times, 11 April, 1981.
(20) Bernard Williams, 'Pathways to the pigeonhole', outline of a paper to the RIPA Conference, April 1981, p.1.
(21) Ibid., pp.2-3.
(22) Rothschild, Random Variables, p.88.
(23) Report to the Departmental Committee on the Procedure of Royal Commissions, Cmnd 5235, HMSO, 1910.
(24) Lord Benson and Lord Rothschild, 'Royal Commissions: A Memorial', Public Administration, Vol. 60, Autumn 1982, pp.339-48.
(25) Ibid., p.340.
(26) Ibid., p.341.
(27) Ibid., p.347.
(28) Ibid., p.348.
(29) See Peter Hennessy and Andrew Arends, 'Whitehall brief: From Domesday to Falklands', The Times, December 14, 1982. The seminar discussion is summarised in Martin Bulmer, Royal Commissions and Departmental Committees of Inquiry, RIPA, 1983.
(30) Hennessy, 'The most elevated and distinguished casualties of the Thatcher years', The Listener, 7 February, 1985.
(31) 'The Good and the Great', BBC Radio 3, February 4, 1985.
(32) Ibid.
(33) Ronald Butt, 'Why Mrs Thatcher could win again', The Times, 20 June 1985.
(34) Ibid.
(35) Thomas (editor), The Establishment, p.191.
(36) David Watt, 'Not old-fashioned - commonsense', The Times, 3 January, 1986.
(37) David Watt, 'Reform the BBC, don't wreck it', The Times, 22 February, 1985.

(38) 'The BBC's own power game', The Observer, 11 August, 1985.
(39) Conversation with Bernard Donoughue, 29 November 1984.
(40) Conversation with Clive Priestley, 28 November 1984.
(41) Richard Hoggart, 'The gravy train runs amok', The Observer, 29 December 1985.
(42) Richard Hoggart, 'Middle ground', New Statesman, 1 February, 1985, pp.31-2.
(43) Hoggart, 'The gravy train runs amok'.
(44) Private information.
(45) Ibid.
(46) Ibid.
(47) See Hennessy, Cabinet, (forthcoming) particularly the chapter on 'Conviction Cabinet, 1979 86'.
(48) Michael Davie, 'Notebook: Inquiring Peacock will dance to his own tune', The Observer, 8 September, 1985, p.44.
(49) I worked with him on The Financial Times and have seen him in action at Ditchley Park.
(50) Ian Aitken, 'Franks "a bucket of whitewash" says scornful Callaghan', The Guardian, 27 January, 1983.
(51) 'The Good and the Great', BBC Radio 3, 4 February 1985.

TOWARDS A NOUVEAU REGIME

It's inevitable that a government is run by an elite. The question is what sort of an elite is it and does it change often enough?
Lord Franks, 1985(1)

The internal dynamics of Westminster, Whitehall and Fleet Street have made second-rate thinking the establishment norm.
Sir John Hoskyns 1983(2)

One's always being told that the bad thing about committees of inquiry and Royal commissions ... is that they are all made up of the same sorts of middle class people. The difficulty I think is to find any other sorts of people who have either the time or the will or the sorts of expertise to be members of these committees.
Lady Warnock, 1985(3)

Patronage is second only to the act of love in conferring pleasure on all parties concerned.
Jonathan Charkham, 1986(4)

One outpost of the G and G that continued to flourish during its years of partial eclipse in Whitehall was Ditchley Park, William Kent's exquisite mansion north of Oxford on the rim of the Cotswolds. There the dispensers of Whitehall patronage such as Sir Robert Armstrong ('he enjoys Eton Collegers' dinners and Ditchley conference weekends'(5)) would mingle with grandees like Lord Franks, scholars, respresentatives of the quality end of Fleet Street, the 'better sort' of politician, a large group of imported Americans of repute and a sprinkling of what musters as a G and G in other Western nations. In such an exquisite setting, to which Churchill would repair on weekends when the moonlight might

ange'(17). The <u>ancien regime</u>, whether it be found among the
...all regulars or their territoral army, the G and G, is no
...enough.

...ne way of putting together a <u>nouveau regime</u> in the shape of
...ry best problem-solving teams without the delay and palaver
...mplicated salary negotiations needed these days to recruit
...outside experts into Whitehall as temporary civil servants
...e to adapt the G and G for the purpose. The idea would be
...outsiders with insiders, Whitehall's own problem-solvers, on
...task force. The team's intellectual firepower, given a bit of
...rming and mutual stimulus, should be greater than the sum
...arts. And when a report or strategy is forthcoming, time
...saved by avoiding the tardy inter-departmental mincing
...which invariably awaits the recommendations of
...tees consisting solely of outsiders. The possibility of
...results flowing from their endeavours should attract busy
...able people in the way that a Royal commission probably no
...an. The G and G in this kind of manifestation could come
...the successful World War II Whitehall model which used
...d so effectively.

...established procedure already exists for putting together
...ces of this type. A section of <u>Questions of Procedure for</u>
...is allotted to it. 'From time to time', it reads,
...tees have been appointed consisting partly of civil servants
...tly of individuals outside the Government with civil
...as chairmen. Any Minister who has it in mind to appoint a
...ee of this kind should consult the Prime Minister'(18). In
...two models which come to mind from the past had expert
...in the chair, both of whom had held permanent secretary
...ier in their careers. The first is Sir William Beveridge's
...ee on social insurance. He presided over a team of
...from seven departments with a wartime temporary from
...omic Section of the Cabinet Office, Sir Norman Chester,
...retary(19). The second was Lord Plowden's committee on
...penditure in the late 1950s. Plowden sat at the end of a
...und which were some of the most formidable Whitehall
...ghts of the day - Sir Burke Trend, Dame Evelyn Sharp, Sir
...ke, Sir Thomas Padmore and Sir Robert Hall assisted by a
...sinessmen(20). Building on the Beveridge and Plowden
...fers the best prospect of all the variants of the G and G
...for combining flexibility, speed, competence and success-
...nentation. It is amazing that it has been so rarely used.
...e adapted for future use quite easily, though it could
...slight rejigging of Dr Morgan's computer categories.

enable the Luftwaffe to bomb Chequers(6), it was possible, with a
dash of romantic imagination, to feel one was back in the era
described by David Cecil. People were careful not to leave open
red boxes in the magnificent library where the plenary sessions
were held. But the sensation of messages humming to and from
Whitehall was real enough. And one recent Ditchley director liked
to close proceedings after the Saturday evening dinner with the
words 'the eighteenth century is now over'(7).

The current director of the Ditchley Foundation, who
watches the G and G ebb and flow from his country park, is Sir
Reginald Hibbert, formerly Ambassador to Paris and Political
Director at the Foreign Office. Almost the <u>ex officio</u> observer in
chief of the Great and the Good, his observations are a good
starting point for any consideration of how best the G and G might
renew themselves if the breed is to have any hope of reaching its
millenium in 2086:

> I don't think the Good and Great do make policy. I don't think
> that is their function. I think they are much like a governor
> on a motor, and it is the motor that makes policy ... What the
> Good and Great do is provide an element of experience and
> continuity, knowledge of what has gone before, knowledge of
> how things are conducted, and they sit there and they talk
> together and they give advice on what is reasonable and
> possible and what isn't. What they do is help to iron out some
> of the excesses of policy and to persuade people that you can
> do a certain number of things at a certain speed, but it's no
> use racing the engine(8).

Listening to Sir Reg it is easy to assign a high place to the G and G
in the fatty bloodstream that has furred up the national arteries
and produced what Mancur Olson has called 'institutional
sclerosis'(9) in a severe form. Professor Dahrendorf, from a
perspective that is part Bonn, part London, sees the dilemma
clearly:

> It's one of those double headed things of which there are
> quite a few. I believe this continuity is quite valuable
> because I came from a country which is characterised by a
> whole series of historical breaks and you don't meet anybody
> who was in before the last historiacal break ... and therefore
> [it] has a very incoherent and non-cohesive elite which has
> something artificial and something ineffective about it.
> Britain, on the other hand, gets to being something like a

closed society by having this kind of establishment ... that is the weakness of it(10).

If one pursues a sanguinary metaphor, the danger is clear - that of endlessly tranfusing the same blood which, however rich, inevitably goes stale. Here lies the clue to replenishment and survival. Given the reluctance of successive administrations to throw open the doors of the career Civil Service to the capable and the innovative on a temporary in-outer basis as was done so successfully between 1939 and 1945, the G and G, a proven, established channel, part of Whitehall's circulatory system, may be the way to introduce new blood into the mainstream. If it is to work, a number of modifications have to be made to the commissioning and recruiting processes.

First of all, rationing would have to be applied and the new G and G called in only when really necessary. Three variants suggest themselves.

(1)	Ground-breaking inquiries in which a corpus of evidence has to be created where little or none already exists.
(2)	Task forces to tackle urgent problems where skill and practical experience are indispensable and amateurism, benevolence and other manifestations of the good chap theory are at a discount.
(3)	Grand, consensus-forming exercises on contentious issues which span parliaments and where cross-party agreement is highly desirable.

From the perspective of a would be reformer in a convention-bound society like ours, the beauty of this trio is that precedents exist for all three.

Ground breakers
This is the grand Victorian marque. 'One thinks of people like Chadwick'(11), says Clive Priestley. 'The Victorian model was one of great intellectual capacity and great moral strength'(12). Given the work of the Central Statistical Office and a small army of contemporary social scientists, it is not obvious at first sight that much scope is left for commissions inquiring into what the Victorians called the condition of England. But occasionally a subject crops up which falls plum into this category. A recent example was Lady Warnock's Departmental Committee on Human Embryology. And Lady Warnock was happy enough to accept her inquiry's categorisation in the Victorian fact-finding class(13). The kind of

team needed for this sort of exercise is a mixtu[...] the balanced all-rounder capable of putting ma[...] Rare resort to this kind of inquiry would [...] authority and respect recent Royal commi[...] Some kind of undertaking to respond and act f[...] of-the-day, along the lines laid down by Be[...] help fill the remaining credibility gap. The[...] Douglas Wass in his 1983 Reith Lectures of [...] Royal Commission with its own staff, which[...] commissions and co-opt members when iss[...] selves, would, among other things, prevent t[...] with rarity(14). The other ingredient re[...] impact is the language in which the finding[...] are conveyed. The Beveridge Report on Soci[...] Services of 1942 offers a salutary lesson her[...] and future wife, Jessy Mair, who, over[...] Edinburgh, encouraged him to imbue the dr[...] statistics of the standard White Paper [...] biographer, Jose Harris, described as 'a "[...] messianic tone'(15). The result was the fiv[...] recovery - Want, Ignorance, Squalor, Idlene[...] which the headline-writers would have beer[...] seller which sold 630,000 copies, a linguis[...] which no official publication on social po[...] near matching since. The Mrs Mair fa[...] Morgan has called 'the dramatic impulse [...] vital to any kind of G and G production.[...] Civil Service draftsmanship and you are lo[...] doubt it, consider for a moment how [...] rewritten the Sermon on the Mount - 'B[...] they shall inherit the earth, from time[...] special circumstances as laid down by mi[...] mind overall expenditure targets'.

Task forces
Here lies the most fertile territory for[...] towards their tenth century. The tim[...] jettison the 'governor on the motor' role[...] congenial Ditchley host, Sir Reg Hibbe[...] already has sufficient arresting facto[...] reckless progress, most notably the C[...] after leaving government, Mrs Shirley [...] tably as 'a beautifully designed and e[...] [which] produces a hundred well argue[...]

Building a successful team of skilled people would be the overriding premium. The careful balancing of institutional representation, genders and regions presided over by a gifted all-rounder good at managing committees would be self-defeating in task force terms. In such cases, meritocracy might be made a conspicuous virtue if the credentials of each member of the task force were displayed in the press release announcing its commissioning.

Consensus builders
There is, however, a genuine if residual role for the old style representational committee. The problems with this sort of body are clear enough. As Ralf Dahrendorf expressed it:

> One sets up a commission in order to defer a decision, certainly defer an uninformed decision. There is a point after about eighteen months where the entire commission seems agreed on some reasonable cause of action and they all like each other very much and go out for weekends, and so on. And it is only when the final report is written and people suddenly remember that they belong to a trade union here, or to a professional organisation there ... and, therefore, cannot possibly sign the report without writing some dissenting opinion ... so the thing falls apart again towards the end(21).

So what on earth is the value of these exercises in getting to know you? 'I have always thought the main point', said Professor Dahrendorf, 'is the process rather than the result'(22).

If the consensus-building model is to be revived, surely such expensive and futile encounter groups must be avoided. For in some cases, they are the most sensible instrument to deploy as even that arch antagonist of the Establishment, Dr Owen, recognises:

> Because it's been cheapened just recently because of too much political interference, [it] does not mean there is not a role for an independent commission. Big constitutional changes, major, far-reaching tax reform changes, which really must begin to stick more in this country ... can often best be developed on the basis of a substantive major report(23).

The examples Dr Owen cited were the Greater London Council, local government reform generally, local government finance and devolution, 'the whole of the constitutional framework in Britain has been done in a frightfully politically and arbitrary partisan fashion, [and] we are reaping the whirlwind'(24). Again consensus building committees must be used carefully and sparingly and never as merely delaying devices.

The greatest and enduring defence of the Royal commission and committee of Inquiry is that they represent a country's commitment to evidence, analysis and reason in the conduct of public affairs, to 'the duty', as the Haldane Report put it as long ago as 1918, 'of investigation and thought as preliminary to action'(25). As such they cannot be expected to flourish in an era of conviction politcs when the mobilisation of political will and prejudice is at a premium and much else is secondary. But the commissions and committees of old England and the great and good who staffed them were well into a period of decay, decline and occasional downright futility long before 1979. In an unreformed condition there is no reason to suppose that a more traditional style of government would inevitably return to them as an instrument of public policy advice. It cannot be taken for granted that there'll always be an England while there's the Good and Great. But with a degree of retooling, a set of revised specifications, a renewed search for new people as the generation of wartime temporaries finally passes and a careful rationing of their use, the G and G could enjoy a late twentieth century revival to the benefit of themselves, Whitehall, the Cabinet and the quality of policy-making generally.

Footnotes
(1) 'The Good and the Great', BBC Radio 3, 4 February, 1985.
(2) Sir John Hoskyns, 'Conservatism is not enough', Institute of Directors Annual Lecture, 28 September, 1983.
(3) 'The Good and the Great', BBC Radio 3, 4 February, 1985.
(4) Jonathan Charkham, 'Board Structure and Appointments in the Public and Private Sectors', 14 February, 1986.
(5) Max Hastings, 'Profile: The muscial mandarin who held the stage', The Sunday Times, 9 February, 1986.
(6) Ronald Tree, When the Moon was High, Memoirs of Peace and War (1887-1942, Macmillan, 1975.
(7) Private information.
(8) 'The Good and the Great', BBC Radio 3, 4 February, 1985.
(9) Mancur Olson, The Rise and Decline of Nations, Economic Growth, Stagflation and Social Rigidities, Yale, 1982, p.78.
(10) 'The Good and the Great', BBC Radio 3, 4 February, 1985.
(11) For an excellent short account of Chadwick and the Royal

74

Commission of Inquiry into the Poor Law of 1832 see Rudolf Klein, 'Edwin Chadwick, 1800-90' in Paul Barker (editor), Founders of the Welfare State, Heinemann, 1984, pp.8-16.

(12)   'The Good and the Great', BBC Radio 3, 4 February, 1985.

(13)   Ibid.

(14)   Douglas Wass, Government and the Governed, Routledge, 1984, pp.112-18. Sir Douglas's most recent thoughts on this theme can be found in a paper he prepared for an RIPA seminar 'A Constitutional Commission for Britain'? held on 3 April, 1985.

(15)   Jose Harris, William Beveridge, A Biography, Oxford University Press, 1977, p.386.

(16)   Kenneth O. Morgan, 'The state of welfare', New Society, 7 February, 1986.

(17)   Shirley Williams, 'The Decision Makers' in Policy and Practice, RIPA, 1980, p.81.

(18)   Private information.

(19)   Harris, William Beveridge, pp.384-5.

(20)   Private information.

(21)   'The Good and the Great', BBC Radio 3, 4 February, 1985.

(22)   Ibid.

(23)   Ibid.

(24)   Ibid.

(25)   Ministry of Reconstruction. Report of the Machinery of Government Committee. Cd. 92 30, HMSO, 1918, p.6.

APPENDIX ONE

ROYAL COMMISSIONS AND COMMITTEES OF INQUIRY, 1945-85

COMMITTEE	CHAIRMAN	FINISH
1945		
The Boarding Out of the O'Neill Boys	Sir Walter Monckton KC	1945
The Selling Price of Houses	John W. Morris KC	1945
Training for Business Administration	Sir Frank Newson-Smith	1945
The Census of Production	Sir George Nelson	1945
China Clay	Professor W.R. Jones	1945
The Census of Distribution	Sir Richard Hopkins	1945
Exhibitions and Fairs	Lord Ramsden	1945
The Remuneration of General Practitioners	Sir Will Spens	1945
Scientific Man-Power	Sir Alan Barlow	1945
Social and Economic Research	Sir John Clapham	1946
New Towns	Lord Reith of Stonehaven	1946
Homeless Children (Scotland)	James L. Clyde KC	1946
Care of Children	Miss Myra Curtis	1946
Legal Aid and Legal Advice in Scotland	John Cameron KC	1946
Electoral Registration	G.H. Oliver, MP	1946
Double Day-Shift Working	Professor J.L. Brierly	1947
1946		
The Case of Arthur Clatworthy	Tom Eastham KC	1946
A Case Heard by Gilling East Justices	Lord Justice Tucker	1946
The Disaster at Bolton Football Ground	R. Moelwyn Hughes KC	1946
The Assessment of Disablement	Judge Ernest Hancock	1946

COMMITTEE	CHAIRMAN	FINISH
The Regent's Park Terraces	Lord Gorell	1947
Expenses of Members of Local Authorities	Lord Lindsay of Birker	1947
The Fire at Merthyr House, Cardiff	John Flowers KC	1946
The Case of John Elliott	J.C. Jolly KC	1946
Procedure in Matrimonial Causes	Mr Justice Denning	1947
The Fire at Ferring Grange Hotel	A.P.L. Sullivan	1947
The Remuneration of General Dental Practitioners	Sir Will Spens	1948
Milk Distribution	Maj-Gen W.D.A. Williams	1948
Justices of the Peace	Lord du Parcq	1948
Army and Air Force Courts-Marshall	Mr Justice Lewis	1948
Mineral Development	Lord Westwood	1949
Shops and Non-Industrial Employment	Sir Ernest Gowers	1949
Awards to Inventors	Sir Lionel Cohen	1956

1947

The Confession Made by David Ware	J.C. Jolly KC	1947
Proceedings before Aberayron Justices	Lord Justice Tucker	1947
Disturbances at Standon Farm Approved School	John C. Maude KC, MP	1947
The Tenure of Shop Premises in Scotland	Prof. T.M. Taylor	1947
The British Film Institute	Sir Cyril Radcliffe KC	1948
The Remuneration of Consultants and Specialists	Sir Will Spens	1948
The Fire at Townshend Terrace	Alfred J. Long KC	1948
Tudor Aircraft	A/C/M Sir C. Courtney	1948
Industrial Diseases	Judge Edgar T. Dale	1948
Mining Subsidence	Theodore Turner KC	1949
County Court Procedure	Mr Justice Jones	1949
Resale Price Maintenance	G.H. Lloyd Jacob KC	1949
The Press	Sir David Ross	1949
Civil Aircraft Certification	A/C W. Helmore	1948

COMMITTEE	CHAIRMAN	FINISH
Civil Aviation Personnel	G/C C.A.B. Wilcock	1948
Children and the Cinema	Professor K.C. Wheare	1950
Land Drainage (Scotland)	Joseph F. Duncan	1949
The From of Government Accts	W.F. Crick	1950
Cremation	D.L. Bateson/H.L. Strutt	1950
Supreme Court Practice and		
Procedure	Lord Justice Evershed	1953

1948

Evasions of Petrol Rationing	G. Russell Vick	1948
Land Registration in		
Scotland	Lord Macmillan	
The Electricity Peak Load		
Problem	Sir Andrew Clow	1948
Medical Partnerships	Mr Justice Slade	1948
Marriage Guidance Grants	Sir Sidney Harris	1948
Higher Civil Service Remun-		
eration	Lord Chorley	1948
Depositions	Mr Justice Byrne	1948
The Political Activities of		
Civil Servants	J.C. Masterman	1949
Taxation & Overseas Minerals	Sir Eric Bamford	1949
The Limitation of Actions	Lord Justice Tucker	1949
Police Conditions of Service	Lord Oaksey	1949
The Cost of the Home Infor-		
mation Services	Sir Henry French	1949
The Distribution and Exhibition		
of Cinematograph Films	Viscount Portal/Professor	
	Sir Arnold Plant	1949
The Tenure of Shops and Business		
Premises in Scotland	Lord Guthrie KC	1949
Illegal Fishing in Scotland	Robert H. Maconochie KC	1949
Celluloid Storage	J.I. Wall	1959
Leasehold in England & Wales	Lord Uthwatt/Lord Justice	
	Jenkins	1950
The Employment of Children in		
Entertainments	Sir Maurice Holmes	1950
The Qualifications of		
Planners	Sir George Schuster	1959
Weights and Measures Legis-		
lation	Sir Edward Hodgson	1950

COMMITTEE	CHAIRMAN	FINISH
Social Workers in the Mental Health Services	Prof. J.M. Mackintosh	1951
Punishments in Prisons, Etc.	H.W.F. Franklin	1951
Scottish Local Government Law Consolidation	Prof. M.G. Fisher QC	1953

1949

The Export and Slaughter of Horses	Earl of Rosebery	1949
Intermediaries	Sir Edwin Herbert	1949
Broadcasting	Lord Radcliffe/Lord Beveridge	1950
The Naval Discipline Act	Mr Justice Pilcher	1950
The Law of Succession in Scotland	Lord Mackintosh	1950
The Industrial Health Services	Judge Edgar T. Dale	1950
Medical Auxiliaries	Dr V. Zachary Cope, MD	1950
The Taxation of Trading Profits	James M. Tucker KC	1951
Betting, Lotteries and Gaming	Sir Henry Willink KC	1951
Cruelty to Wild Animals	J. Scott Henderson KC	1951
Local Land Charges	Sir John Stainton KC	1951
State Immunities	Lord Justice Somervell	1951
The Statutory Registration of Opticians	Lord Crook	1952
Capital Punishment	Sir Ernest Gowers	1953
The Supreme Court of Northern Ireland	Lord Justice Black/Mr Justice Sheil	1957

1950

Aircraft Landing and Taking-Off	Lord Brabazon of Tara	1951
Stoppages in the London Dock	Sir Frederick Leggett	1951
The Law of Intestate Succession	Lord Morton of Henryton	1951
The Court of Record for the Hundred of Salford	G.R. Upjohn KC	1951

COMMITTEE	CHAIRMAN	FINISH
Night Baking	Sir Frederick Rees	1951
Scottish Financial and Trade Statistics	Lord Catto	1952
Charitable Trusts	Lord Nathan	1952
The Taxation of Provisions for Retirement	James M. Tucker KC	1953
Report of the Committee on Maladjusted Children	Dr J.E.A. Underwood	1955

1951

Purchase Tax/Utility	Sir William Douglas	1951
A Draft Customs and Excise Bill	Lord Kennet of the Dene	1951
Post Office Recognition	Sir Maurice Holmes/Lord Terrington	1952
Cotton Import	Sir Richard Hopkins	1952
University Education in Dundee	Lord Tedder	1952
The National Museum of Antiquities of Scotland	J.R. Philip QC	1952
The Use of Fuel and Power Resources	Viscount Ridley	1952
Scottish Leases	Lord Guthrie	1952
Welsh Language Publishing	A.W. Ready	1952
Copyright	Marquess of Reading/H.S. Gregory	1952
Liability for Damage Done by Animals	Lord Chief Justice Goddard	1952
Discharged Prisoners' Aid Societies	Sir Alexander Maxwell	1953
Crofting Conditions	Principal Thomas Murray	1954
Drainage of Trade Premises	Lord Hill Watson QC	1954
The Taxation of Profits and Income	Sir Lionel Cohen/Lord Radcliffe	1955
Marriage and Divorce	Lord Morton of Henryton	1955

1952

The Conviction of Devlin Burns	Albert D. Gerrard QC	1952
Security Arrangements at Broadmoor	J. Scott Henderson QC	1952
Tax-Paid Stocks	Sir Maurice Hutton	1953

79

COMMITTEE	CHAIRMAN	FINISH
The Taxicab Service	Viscount Runciman of Doxford	1953
Purchase Tax (Valuation)	Frederick Grant QC	1953
Entry into Certain Branches of the Royal Navy	Ewen E.S. Montagu QC	1953
The Slaughter of Horses	Duke of Northumberland	1953
A New Criminal Court in South Lancashire	Sir Alexander Maxwell	1953
Shares of No Par Value	Montagu L. Gedge QC	1954
Recruitment and Publicity for Civil Defence	William Mabane	1954
The Overseas Information Services	Earl of Drogheda	1954
New Trials in Criminal Cases	Lord Tucker	1954
Departmental Records	Sir James Grigg	1954
Scottish Affairs	Earl of Balfour	1954
Foot-and-Mouth Disease	Sir Ernest Gowers	1954
Close Seasons for Deer in Scotland	Robert H. Maconochie QC	1954

1953

Cotton Import (Review)	Sir Richard Hopkins	1953
The Case of Timothy John Evans	J. Scott Henderson QC	1953
Coastal Flooding	Viscount Waverley	1954
The Disposal of Land at Crichel Down	Sir Andrew Clark QC	1954
Scottish Valuation & Rating	Lord Sorn	1954
The Adoption of Children	Sir Gerald Hurst QC	1954
The Censuses of Production and Distribution	Sir Reginald Verdon-Smith	1954
Air Pollution	Sir Hugh Beaver	1954
The Problems of Providing for Old Age	Sir Thomas Phillips	1954
Slaughterhouses (Scotland)	Sir John Handford	1954
Mathematics and Science Teachers in Scotland	Sir Edward Appleton	1955
East Africa	Sir Hugh Dow	1955
Slaughterhouses (England and Wales)	R. Herbert	1955
Statutory Provisions for Industrial Diseases	F.W. Beney QC	1955

COMMITTEE	CHAIRMAN	FINISH
The Civil Service	Sir Raymond Priestley	1955
The Cost of the National Health Service	C.W. Guillebaud	1955
Disabled Persons	Lord Piercy	1956

1954

COMMITTEE	CHAIRMAN	FINISH
Local Objections to Gatwick Airport	Sir Colin Campbell	1954
The Transfer of Certain Civil Servants	J.H. Woods	1954
Boys' Units in the Army	B.L. Hallward	1955
A New Queen's Hall	Professor Lionel Robbins	1955
Crown Lands	Sir M. Trustram Eve	1955
The Territorial Army	J.R.H. Hutchison MP/ Fitzroy Maclean	1955
The Summary Trial of Minor Offences	Sir Reginald Sharpe QC	1955
The Electricity Supply Industry	Sir Edwin Herbert	1955
The Local Organisation of the Ministry of Agriculture, Fisheries and Food	Sir Arton Wilson	1956
The Office of the Public Trustee	Sir Maurice Holmes	1955
Land Charges	Mr Justice Roxburgh	1956
Law relating to Mental Illness and Mental Deficiency	Lord Percy of Newcastle	1957
Homosexual Offences and Prostitution	Sir John Wolfenden	1957
Building Legislation in Scotland	C.W. Graham Guest QC	1957
Committee on Transactions in Seeds Plant Breeders Rights	B.C. Engholm	1954

1955

COMMITTEE	CHAIRMAN	FINISH
Pig Production	Sir Harold Howitt	1955
Security	Marquess of Salisbury	1956
A Department of Scientific and Industrial Research	Sir Harry Jephcott	1955
The Employment of Children in the Potato Harvest	Sir Hugh Rose	1956
The Composition and Nutritive Value of Flour	Prof. Sir Henry Cohen	1956

COMMITTEE	CHAIRMAN	FINISH
Unpatented Inventions in		
Defence Contracts	Sir Harold Howitt	1956
The Dock Workers Scheme, 1947	Mr Justice Devlin	1956
Recruitment to the Dental		
Profession	Lord McNair QC	1956
Cheque Endorsement	A.A. Macatta QC	1956
Horticultural Marketing	Viscount Runciman of	
	Doxford	1956
Administrative Tribunals and		
Inquiries	Sir Oliver Franks	1957
Bankruptcy Law Amendment	Judge John B. Blagden	1957
Common Land	Sir Ivor Jennings QC	1958
Hallmarking and Assaying	Sir Leonard Stone	1958

1956

The Employment of National		
Service Men	J.F. Wolfenden	1956
Welsh Broadcasting	Sir Godfrey Ince	1956
Damage and Casualties in		
Port Said	Sir Edwin Herbert	1956
The Army Cadet Force	Fitzroy Maclean MP/	
	Julian Amery MP	1957
Coal Distribution Costs	Sir Thomas Robson	1958
Diligence	Sheriff Hector McKechnie	1958
Inland Waterways	H. Leslie Bowes	1958
Ill-treatment of Prisoners in		
Liverpool Prison	Sir Godfrey Vick QC	1956
Children and Young People	Viscount Ingleby	1960
Smithfield Market: causes of		
Industrial Unrest	R.M. Wilson QC	1956
The supply and training of		
teachers for technical		
colleges: report of a		
special committee appointed		
by the Minister of Educ-		
ation in September 1956	Mr Willis Jackson	1957
Qualifications of Teachers in		
Schools holding the Teacher's		
Technical Certificate	H.H. Donnelly	1956

COMMITTEE	CHAIRMAN	FINISH

1957

COMMITTEE	CHAIRMAN	FINISH
The Export of Live Cattle for Slaughter	Lord Balfour of Burleigh	1957
The Carlisle State Management Scheme	C.S.S. Burt QC	1957
The Cardiganshire Constabulary	H.J. Phillmore	1957
The Purchasing Procedure of the British Transport Commission	Sir Harold Howitt	1957
The Interception of Communications	Sir Norman Birkett	1957
The Organisation of the Atomic Energy Authority	Sir Alexander Fleck	1957
Health and Safety in the Atomic Energy Authority	Sir Alexander Fleck	1957
The Preservation of Downing Street	Earl of Crawford and Balcarres	1958
The Windscale Piles	Sir Alexander Fleck	1958
The Rights of Light	Mr Justice Harman	1958
Proceedings before Examining Justices	Lord Tucker	1958
Conditions in the Prison Services	Mr Justice Wynn-Parry	1958
Recruiting for the Armed Forces	Sir James Grigg	1958
Grassland Utilisation	Sir Sydney Caine	1958
Further Education for Agriculture	Earl De La Warr	1958
The Public Library Service	Sir Sydney Roberts	1958
London Roads	G.R.H. Nugent MP	1959
The Working of the Monetary System	Lord Radcliffe	1959
Anthrax	R.F. Levy QC	1959
Civil Jury Trial in Scotland	Lord Strachan	1959
Doctors' and Dentists' Remuneration	Sir Harry Pilkington	1960
Legal Aid in Criminal Proceedings	Lord Guthrie	1960
Local Government in Greater London	Sir Edwin Herbert	1960
The Fishing Industry	Sir Alexander Fleck	1960
Salmon and Freshwater Fisheries	B.L. Bathurst	1961

83

COMMITTEE	CHAIRMAN	FINISH

1958

The Tenancy of Shops (Scotland) Act, 1949	Ian H. Shearer QC	1958
The Misuse of Official Facilities	Sir Norman Brook	1958
The Disposal of Scrap Cable by the London Electricity Board	Henry Benson	1958
Highway Law Consolidation	Marquess of Reading	1958
Matrimonial Proceedings in Magistrates' Courts	Mr Justice Arthian Davies	1958
Co-operation between Area and Scottish Electricity and Gas Boards	Sir Cecil Weir	1959
Funds in Court	Mr Justice Pearson	1959
The Rating of Charities	Sir Fred Pritchard	1959
Conflicts of Jurisdiction Affecting Children	Lord Justice Hodson	1959
Caravans as Homes	Sir Arton Wilson	1959
The Youth Service in England and Wales	Countess of Albemarle	1959
Chancery Chambers and the Chancery Rgistrar's Office	Lord Justice Harman	1960
Grants to Students	Sir Colin Anderson	1960
Human Artificial Insemination	Earl of Feversham	1960
Milk Composition	J.W. Cook	1960
The Examination of Steam Boilers in Industry	G.G. Honeyman	1960
The Business of the Criminal Courts	Mr Justice Streatfield	1960
Local Contributions to the Scottish Universities	The Hon. Lord Sorn MC	1959

1959

The Colonial Development Corporation	Lord Sinclair of Cleeve	1959
Disturbances at Carlton Approved School	Victor Durand QC	1959
Solid Smokeless Fuels	N.M. Peech	1960
A Levy on Betting on Horse Races	L.E. Peppiatt	1960

84

COMMITTEE	CHAIRMAN	FINISH
Coal Derivatives	A.H. Wilson	1960
The Importation of Charollais Cattle	Lord Terrington	1960
Compensation for Victims of Crimes of Violence	(chairman unknown)	1960
The Control of Public Expenditure	Lord Plowden	1961
The Remuneration of Milk Distributors	Sir Guy Thorold	1961
Company Law	Lord Jenkins	1962
Consumer Protection	J.T. Molony QC	1962
The Probation Service	Sir Ronald Morison QC	1962
Industrial Designs	Kenneth Johnston QC	1962
Scottish Licensing Law	Lord Guest	1963
The Registration of Title to Land in Scotland	Lord Reid	1963
Truck Acts	David Karmel	1961
Conflicts of Jurisdiction affecting children	Lord Hodson	1959

1960

Powers of Subpoena of Disciplinary Tribunals	Viscount Simonds	1960
Legal Education for African Students	Lord Denning	1960
Magistrates Courts in London	Judge C.D. Arnold	1961
Fowl Pest Policy	Prof. Sir Arnold Plant	1962
The Police	Sir Henry Willink QC	1962
Broadcasting	Sir Harry Pilkington	1962
The Problem of Noise	Sir Alan Wilson	1963
Ocean Shipowners' Tally Clerks; difficulties in Port of London	H. Lloyd-Williams	1960
The teaching of Russian: report of the committee appointed by the Minister of Education and the Secretary of State for Scotland in September 1960	Mr N.G. Annan	1962

COMMITTEE	CHAIRMAN	FINISH

1961

Security in the Public Service	Lord Radcliffe	1961
Security at the National Gallery	Lord Bridges	1962
The Press	Lord Shawcross QC	1962
The Major Ports of Great Britain	Viscount Rochdale	1962
The Limitation of Actions for Personal Injury	Mr Justice E. Davies	1962
The Economy of Northern Ireland	Sir Herbert Brittain/ Sir Robert Hall	1962
Electricity in Scotland	C.H. Mackenzie	1962
The Teaching Profession in Scotland	Lord Wheatley	1963
Decimal Currency	Earl of Halsbury	1963
Higher Education	Professor Lord Robbins	1963
Children and Young Persons (Scotland)	Lord Kilbrandon	1964
The Law on Sunday Observance	Lord Crathorne	1964
Arrangements for the Award & Withdrawal of Certificates of Competency to Teach	Rt. Hon Lord Wheatley	1961

1962

The Vassall Case	Sir Charles Cunningham	1962
The Organisation of Civil Science	Sir Burke Trend	1963
Representational Services Overseas	Lord Plowden	1963
Meat Marketing and Distribution	Sir Reginald Verdon-Smith	1964
Overseas Geology & Mining	Sir Frederick Brundrett	1963
The Demand for Agricultural Graduates	C.I.C. Bonsanquet	1964
Recruitment for the Veterinary Profession	Duke of Northumberland	1964
Generation & Distribution of Electricity in Scotland	C.H. MacKenzie	1962
Scottish Salmon and Trout Fisheries	Lord Hunter	1965
National Incomes	Mr F.G. Lawrence	1965

COMMITTEE	CHAIRMAN	FINISH
Day Release: the report of a committee set up by the Minister of Education	Mr C. Henniker-Heaton	1964

1963

The Security Service and Mr Profumo	Lord Denning	1963
A Complaint by the National Union of Bank Employees	Lord Cameron QC	1963
Turnover Taxation	Gordon Richardson	1964
The Case of Mr Herman Woolf	Norman J. Skelhorn	1964
The Renumeration of Ministers and MPs	Sir Geoffrey Lawrence	1964
The Impact of Rates on Households	Prof. R.G.D. Allen	1964
Housing in Greater London	Sir Milner Holland QC	1965
Jury Service	Lord Morris of Borth-y-Gest	1965
Experiments on Animals	Sir Sydney Littlewood	1965
Social Studies	Lord Heyworth	1965
Positive Covenants Affecting Land	Mr Justice Wilberforce	1965
The Legal Status of the Welsh Language	Sir David Hughes Parry	1965
Legal Records	Lord Denning	1966
The Sheriff Court	Lord Grant	1967
Statutory Smallholdings	Prof. M.J. Wise	1967
Criminal Statistics	Wilfrid Perks	1967
Criminal Statistics in Scotland	Alexander Thomson QC	1968
London Transport Board's Road Services, Pay & Conditions of Drivers & Conductors jointly with Minister of Transport)	Henry Phelps Brown	1964
Yorkshire Area of the Coalmining Industry, difference involving Yorkshire Winding Enginemen's Association & National Union of Mineworkers, and National Coal Board	Sir Roy Wilson QC	1964

COMMITTEE	CHAIRMAN	FINISH

Children and their primary
  schools: a report of the
  Central Advisory Council
  for Education (England).
  Vol. I: Research and

| Surveys, 1963 | Lady Bridget Plowden | 1967 |

Inquiry held by the Visiting
  Committee into Allegations
  of Ill-treatment of

| Prisoners at HMP Durham | Mr T.R. Perch | 1963 |

1964

The Cases of Halloran and		
Cox and others	W.L. Mars-Jones QC	1964
Ministry of Aviation Contracts	Sir John Lang	1965
Licensing Planning	J. Ramsay Willis QC	1965
The Port Transport Industry	Lord Devlin	1965
The Court of Criminal Appeal	Lord Donovan	1965
The Welfare of Livestock	Prof. F.W.R. Brambell	1965
The Assessment of Disablement	Lord McCorquodale	1965
The Aircraft Industry	Lord Plowden	1965
Legal Aid in Criminal Pro-		
ceedings	Mr Justice Widgery	1966
The Penal System	Viscount Amory	1966
The Law of Succession by		
Illegitimate Persons	Lord Justice Russell	1966
The Mechanical Recording of		
Court Proceedings	Mr Justice Baker	1966
Conveyancing Legislation and		
Practice	Prof. J.M. Halliday	1966
General Medical Services in		
the Highlands & Islands	Lord Birsay	1967
Dispute at Spitalfields,		
Borough, Stratford, Brent-		
ford and King's Cross		
Markets (jointly with		
Minister of Agriculture,		
Fisheries & Food)	D.T. Jack	1964
The education of deaf children:		
the possible place of finger		
spelling and signing: report		

COMMITTEE	CHAIRMAN	FINISH
of the committee appointed by the Secretary of State for Education and Science in October 1964	Professor M.M. Lewis	1968
Aberdeen Typhoid Outbreak	Sir David Milne GCB	1984
Conveyancing Legislation & Practice (Scotland)	Prof. J.M. Halliday MA	1966

1965

COMMITTEE	CHAIRMAN	FINISH
The Bossard and Allen Cases	Sir Henry Wilson Smith	1965
Shipbuilding	A.R.M. Geddes	1966
The Case of Timothy John Evans	Mr Justice Brabin	1966
The Age of Majority	Mr Justice Latey	1967
The Pharmaceutical Industry	Lord Sainsbury	1967
Medical Education	Professor Lord Todd	1968
Trade Unions and Employers' Associations	Lord Donovan QC	1968
Local Authority Personal Social Services	Frederic Seebohm	1968
The Enforcement of Judgement Debts	Mr Justice Payne	1968
A Scheme for the Registration of Title to Land in Scotland	Prof. G.L.F. Henry	1969
Allotments	Professor H. Thorpe	1969
Death Certification and Coroners	Norman Brodrick QC	1971
Difference between two sides of National Council for the Omnibus Industry	Sir Roy Wilson QC	1965
Prices and Incomes	Rt. Hon Aubrey Jones	1967
Enquiry into the flow of candidates in science and technology into higher education, 1965	Dr F.S. Dainton	1968
Public Schools Commmission. First Report, Vol. I: Report Vol. II: Appendices 1965	Sir John Newsom	1968
A review of the scope and problems of scientific and technological manpower policy, 1965	Prof. Sir Willis Jackson	1965

COMMITTEE	CHAIRMAN	FINISH

Report on education and training
  requirements for the electrical
  and mechanical manufacturing
  industries, 1965 — Mr G.S. Bosworth — 1966
Measures to Secure a more
  Equitable Distribution
  of Teachers in Scotland — Dame Jean Roberts DBE — 1966

1966

Pay for Dock Workers — Lord Devlin — 1966
Tribunals of Inquiry — Lord Justice Salmon QC — 1966
Prison Escapes & Security — Earl Mountbatten of Burma — 1966
Immigration Appeals — Sir Roy Wilson QC — 1967
Statutory Maintenance Limits — Miss Jean Graham Hall — 1968
The Civil Service — Lord Fulton — 1968
Civil Judicial Statistics — Chief Master Paul Adams — 1968
Personal Injuries Litigation — Lord Justice Winn — 1968
Herbage Seed Supplies — C.H.M. Wilcox/Lord
  — Donaldson — 1968
The Protection of Field
  Monuments — Sir David Walsh — 1969
Local Government in England — Sir John Redcliffe-Maud — 1969
Local Government in Scotland — Lord Wheatley QC — 1969
Assizes and Quarter Sessions — Lord Beeching — 1969
The Supreme Court of Judicature
  of Northern Ireland — Lord MacDermott KC — 1969
Dispute between Steel Company
  of Wales and Amalgamated
  Union of Building Trade
  Workers — Prof. D.J. Robertson — 1966
Committee on Football, 1966 — Mr D. Norman Chester — 1968
A report on the supply and
  training of librarians — Mr F.W. Jessup — 1968

1967

'D' Notice Matters — Lord Radcliffe — 1967
Punishment at Court Lees
  Approved School — Edward B. Gibbens QC — 1967
The Accident to the Drilling
  Rig Sea Gem — J. Roland Adams QC — 1967

90

COMMITTEE	CHAIRMAN	FINISH
Capital Projects Overseas	Earl of Cromer	1968
Labour in Building and Civil Engineering	Prof. E.H. Phelps Brown	1968
Intermediate Areas	Sir Joseph Hunt	1969
Marriage Law in Scotland	Lord Kilbrandon QC	1969
Civil Air Transport	Prof. Sir Ronald Edwards	1969
National Libraries	Dr F.S. Dainton	1969
Contempt of Tribunals of Enquiry	Lord Justice Salmon QC	1969
Shipping	Viscount Rochdale	1970
The Fire Service	Sir Ronald Holroyd	1970
The Patent System and Patent Law	M.A.L. Banks	1970
Scottish Inshore Fisheries	Hon.Lord Cameron QC	1970
The London Taxicab Trade	Hon. A. Maxwell Stamp	1970
Legal Education	Hon. Mr Justice Ormrod QC	1971
Primary Education in Wales	Prof. C.E. Gittins	1967
Report of the Reorganisation Commission for Eggs	R. Wright	1968
Committee of Inquiry into Allegations of ill-treatment of patients and other irregularities at the Ely Hospital, Cardiff	Mr Geoffrey Howe QC	1969

1968

Delays in CEGB Power Stations	Sir Alan Wilson	1969
Overseas Representation	Sir Val Duncan	1969
Trawler Safety	Admiral Sir Derec Holland-Martin	1969
Method II Section of Administrative Class Civil Servants	J.G.W. Davies	1969
Antibiotics in Animal Husbandry and Veterinary Medicine	Prof. Michael M. Swann	1969
Foot-and-Mouth Disease	Duke or Northumberland	1969
Commercial Rating	Prof. D.S. Anderson	1970
Consumer Credit	Lord Crowther	1970
Compulsory Retirement Age of Dock Workers	J.S. Wordie	1968
Public Schools Commission. Second report. Vol. I & II.		

COMMITTEE	CHAIRMAN	FINISH
Report on independent day schools and direct grant grammar schools, Vol. III: Scotland, 1968	Professor D.V. Donnison	1970
The Education of the Visually Handicapped: Report of the Committee of Enquiry 1968	Prof. M.D. Vernon	1972
Moral & Religious Education in Scottish Schools	Prof. W. Malcolm Millar	1972
Commercial Rating (Scotland)	Prof. D.S. Anderson	1970

1969

An Education Dispute in Durham	Dr W.E.J. McCarthy	1969
The Functions and Organisation of the Central Training Council	Frank Cousins	1970
Boy Entrants and Young Service-men	Lord Donaldson	1970
The Rent Acts	H.E. Francis QC	1971
Medical and Toxicological Aspects of CS	Sir Harold Himsworth	1971
Small Firms	J.E. Bolton	1971
Adoption of Children	Sir William Houghton/ Judge F.A. Stockdale	1972
The Constitution	Lord Crowther/Lord Kilbrandon	1973
One-Parent Families	Sir Morris Finer	1974
Difference between Newlyn Pier & Harbour Commissioners & Transport & General Workers' Union	Prof. W. Hagenbuch	1970
Industrial Relations	Mr George Woodcock	1971
Adult Education: A plan for development. Report of a Committee of Inquiry	Sir Lionel Russel	1973
Speech therapy services: report of the committee 1969	Professor R. Quirk	1972
Training of Staff for Centres for the Mentally Handi-capped (Scotland)	Charles Melville MA MEd	1973

COMMITTEE	CHAIRMAN	FINISH
The death of David Tomlinson at Paddington General Hospital in July 1967	D.J. Stinson	not known

1970

COMMITTEE	CHAIRMAN	FINISH
Industrial Relations at Heathrow Airport	Prof. D.R. Robertson/ W.H. Griffiths QC	1970
Defence Procurement	D.G. Rayner	1971
Rabies	R. Waterhouse QC	1971
Privacy	K. Younger	1972
Safety and Health at Work	Lord Robens	1972
Nursing	Prof. Asa Briggs	1972
Penalties for Homicide	Lord Emslie	1972
Dispersal of Government Work from London	Sir Henry Hardman	1973
Environmental pollution (permanent)	Sir Eric Ashby/Sir Brian Flowers/Prof. H. Kornberg	permanent
Teaching education & training: report by a committee of inquiry. 1970	Lord James of Rusholme	1972
Adult Education (Scotland)	Prof. K.J.W. Alexander	1975
Secondary Education of Physically Handicapped Children in Scotland	Cllr. P.T. McCann JP BL	1975
Criminal Appeals in Scotland	The Hon. Lord Thomson	1972
Penalties for Homicide (Scotland)	Rt. Hon Lord Emslie	1972
The administration and conditions at Farleigh Hospital	Major Tasker Watkins	1970

1971

COMMITTEE	CHAIRMAN	FINISH
Work of the Fire Service	Sir Charles Cunningham	1971
Allegations of Brutality in N. Ireland	Sir Edmund Compton	1971
Interrogation of Terrorists	Lord Parker of Waddington	1972
Public Trustee Office	H.R. Hutton	1971
Crowd Safety	Lord Wheatley	1972
Future of the Dundee Institute of Art & Technology	Sir Charles H. Wilson	1973

COMMITTEE	CHAIRMAN	FINISH
Work and Pay of Probation Officers and Social Workers	J.B. Butterworth	1972
Contract Farming	Sir James Barker	1972
Section 2 of the Offical Secrets Act, 1911	Lord Franks	1972
Bilingual Traffic Signs	Roderic Bowen QC	1972
Liquor Licensing	Lord Erroll of Hale	1972
Abuse of Social Security Benefits	Hon. Sir Henry Fisher	1972
National Savings	Sir Harry Page	1973
Property Bonds and Equity-linked Life Assurance	Sir Hilary Scott	1973
Scottish Licensing Law	Dr C.W. Clayson	1973
Lotteries	K.P. Witney	1973
The Working of the Abortion Act	Mrs Justice Lane	1974
Dispute between Amalgamated Union of Engineering Workers and Transport & General Workers' Union, and Fine Tubes Ltd	Prof. A.D. Campbell	1971
Provincial Museums & Galleries: a report of a committee appointed by the Paymaster General 1971	Mr C.W. Wright	1973
Report of the Committee of Inquiry into the Veterinary Profession, 1971.	Sir Michael Swann	1975
Civil & Criminal Jurisdiction in N. Ireland. (Commissioned with N. Ireland Sec.	Lord Lowry	1973
Law on Contempt of Court (Commissioned with Lord Advocate)	The Rt. Hon. Sir Henry Josceline Phillimore	1974
Law on Defamation	His Honour Judge Faulks	1975
The administration & conditions at Whittingham Hospital	Sir Robert Payne	1971

1972

Lead Poisonings at Avonmouth Smelter	Sir Brian Windeyer	1972

COMMITTEE	CHAIRMAN	FINISH
Legal Procedures to Deal with Terrorists in N. Ireland	Lord Diplock	1972
Discharge and Supervision of Certain Psychiatric Patients	Sir Carl Aarvold	1972
Children's Footwear	Mrs Alison Munro	1972
The Use of Valuers in the Public Service	R.S. Borner	1973
British Trade Mark Law and Practice	H.R. Mathys	1973
The Export of Animals for Slaughter	Lord O'Brien of Lothbury	1974
The Handling of Complaints against the Police (England and Wales)	A.D. Gordon-Brown	1973
The Handling of Complaints against the Police (Scotland)	W.K. Fraser	1973
Local Government Rules of Conduct	Lord Redcliffe-Maud	1974
Report of the Committee on Legal Education in Northern Ireland	Prof. A.L. Armitage	1973
Report of the Committee on County Courts and Magistrates' Courts in Northern Ireland	Rt. Hon Lord Justice Jones	1973
A Language for Life: Report of the Committee of Inquiry. 1972	Sir Alan Bullock	1975
The Care of Patients at South Ockendon Hospital	J. Hampden Inskip QC	1973
The cause of the fire and action taken at the Coldharbour Hospital on 5 July 1972	Desmond Vowden QC	1972
Medical and nursing practices between 1970 and 1972 in some wards of Napsbury Hospital	Dr R.R. Bomford	1972
Committee on Mentally abnormal offenders	The Rt. Hon. Lord Butler	1975

COMMITTEE	CHAIRMAN	FINISH

1973

Brankruptcy Convention	Kenneth Cork	1976
Copyright and Designs Law	Hon. Mr Justice Whitford	1977
Distribution of business between Crown Courts & Magistrates' Courts	Rt. Hon. Sir Arthur James	1975
Royal Commission on Civil Liability & Compensation for Personal Injury	Lord Pearson	1978
Report of Committee on Rent Restriction Law of Northern Ireland	Hon. Sir Robert Porter QC	1975
Report of the Law Enforcement Commission. To the Secretary of State for N. Ireland & the Minister of Justice of Ireland	None	1974
Report of the Committee of Inquiry into the Disputes involving teachers in the area of the Teeside Local Education Authority	Prof. J.C. Wood	1973
Committee on the Export of Animals for Slaughter	Lord O'Brien of Lothbury	1974
Committee on Broadcasting Coverage	Sir Stewart Crawford	1974
The care and Supervision provided by local authorities and other agencies in relation to Maria Colwell	T.G. Field-Fisher	1974
Conduct in Local Government	Lord Redcliffe-Maud	1974

1974

Local Government Finance	F. Layfield QC	1976
Channel Tunnel and Alternative Cross Channel Services	Sir Alec Cairncross	1975
Reparation by the Offender to the Victim in Scotland	Hon. Lord Dunpark	1977
Truancy & Indiscipline in Schools (Scotland)	Prof. D.C. Park	1977

COMMITTEE	CHAIRMAN	FINISH
Consideration given and Steps taken towards securing the welfare of Richard Clark by Perth Town Council and other Bodies or Persons concerned	C.E. Jauncey QC	1975
Report of a Committee to consider, in the context of civil liberties and human rights, measures to deal with terrorism in Northern Ireland	Rt. Hon. Lord Gardiner	1975
Committee on the Future of Broadcasting	Lord Annan	1974
Assistant in the 3rd and 4th Years of Secondary Education in Scotland	J. Dunning	1974
The Press	Sir Morris Finer/ Professor O McGregor	1977
Distribution of income and personal wealth	Lord Diamond	1979
Standards of Conduct in Public Life	Lord Salmon	1976
Dispute at Odhams (Watford) Ltd	Prof. G.F. Thomason	1974
Report of the Committee of Inquiry into the Pay of Non-University Teachers	Rt. Hon. Lord Houghton	1974
Special education needs: report of the Committee of Enquiry into the education of Handicapped Children and Young People	Mrs H.M. Warnock	1978
British Leyland	Sir Don Ryder	1975
Inflation Accounting	F.E.P. Sandilands	1975
Queens Award to Industry	HRH The Duke of Edinburgh	1975
Committee of Inquiry into water charges in the area of the Welsh National Water Development Authority	Sir Goronwy Daniel	1975

COMMITTEE	CHAIRMAN	FINISH
The cause of the fire at Fairfield House, Edwalton, Notts on 15 December 1974	K.G. Jupp	1975

1975 *

COMMITTEE	CHAIRMAN	FINISH
Committee of Inquiry into the structure of the electricity supply industry in England and Wales	Lord Plowden	1976
Ministerial Memoirs	Viscount Radcliffe	1976
Recruitment of Mercenaries	Lord Diplock	1975
Industrial Democracy	Lord Bullock	1977
Judicial Studies and Information	Lord Bridge	1978
Report of a Committee to Review the Principles and Operations of the Criminal Injuries to Property (Compensation) Act (Northern Ireland) 1971	Sir James Waddell CB	1976
A New partnership for our schools: report of the committee of enquiry	Mr T. Taylor	1977
The nursing and care of the mentally handicapped	Mrs Peggy Jay	1979

1976

COMMITTEE	CHAIRMAN	FINISH
Trunk Road Assessment	Sir George Leitch	1977
Policy Optimisation (Treasury)	Prof. R.J. Ball	1978
Council for the Welsh language	Mr Ben G. Jones	1978
Report on the present and projected financial position of the Northern Ireland Electricity Service	Mr G.T. Shepherd	1976
Rate liability of bodies providing facilites for sport, recreation and		

98

COMMITTEE	CHAIRMAN	FINISH
community activities in Northern Ireland	Prof R.J. Lawrence	1978
Remuneration of Members of Local Authorities	D. Robinson	1977
Legal Services in Scotland	Rt Hon. Lord Hughes	1980
National Health Service	Sir Alec Merrison	1979
Gambling	Lord Rothschild	1978
Personal Injuries Litigation Procedure	Hon. Mr Justice Cantley	1979
Royal Commission on Legal Services (England Wales and N.I.)	Lord Benson	1979
Committee on Data Protection	Sir Norman Lindop	1976

1977

COMMITTEE	CHAIRMAN	FINISH
Committee of Inquiry into the Engineering Profession	Sir Monty Finniston	1979
Opportunities at Sixteen (NI)	Mr Derek Birley	1978
Financing of Small Firms	Sir Harold Wilson	1979
Motorists and Fixed Penalties (Scotland) (First Report by Committee on Alternatives to Prosecution)	Hon. Lord Steward MC	1980
Keeping Offenders out of Court (Second Report by Committee on Alternatives to Prosecution) Scotland	Hon. Lord Steward MC	1983
The Film Industry	Sir Harold Wilson	1977
School examinations: report of the steering committee established to consider proposals for replacing the General Certificate of Education ordinary level and Certificate of Secondary Education examinations by a common system of examining	Sir James Waddell	1978
Motorway Service Areas	Peter J. Prior	1978
Road Haulage Operators' Licensing	Christopher D. Foster	1978

COMMITTEE	CHAIRMAN	FINISH
Committee of Inquiry into Serious Gas Explosions	Mr P.J. King	1977
Review of Rural Planning Policy (NI)	Dr W.H. Cockroft MA	1978
The Functioning of Financial Institutions	Sir Harold Wilson	1980
Committee of Inquiry into the Acquisition and Occupancy of Agricultural Land	Lord Northfield	1979
Committee on Obscenity and Film Censorship	Prof. Bernard Williams	1979
Committee of Inquiry on the Police	Lord Edmund-Davies	1977
Patient Care and Staff Morale at Normansfield Hosp.	M.D. Sherrard QC	1978
Cabinet Document Security	Lord Houghton	1977

1978

Committee on Waste Paper Supply (DI/DOE Jointly)	Dr R.L.P. Berry	1980
The Investigatory Commission into Northern Ireland Housing Executive Contracts	Judge R.T. Rowland QC	1979
Committee of Inquiry into police interrogation procedures in N. Ireland: Report	Judge H.G. Bennett QC	1979
N. Ireland Review Committee on Mental Health Legislation	Mr Justice MacDermott	1981
The Future of Higher Education in N. Ireland - the Report of the Higher Education Review Group for Northern Ireland	Sir Henry Chilver	1982
The non-accidental death of Darryn Clarke	John Hugill QC	1979
Mathematics counts: report of the Committee of Inquiry into the Teaching of Mathematics in Schools. 1978	Dr W.H. Cockroft	1981

COMMITTEE	CHAIRMAN	FINISH
Selection and access to modern public records	Sir Duncan Wilson	1981
The Affairs of Grays Building Society	I.H. Davidson	1979
Criminal procedure	Prof. Sir Cyril Philips	1981
Committee of Inquiry into the UK Prison Services	Sir John Douglas May	1979

1979

Insolvency Law Review Cmtte.	Sir Kenneth Cork	1981
Lorries, People and the Environment	Sir Arthur Armitage	1980
Non-departmental Public Bodies	Sir Leo Pliatzky	1980
Treatment of children with cancer at the Royal Manchester Children's Hosp. & the Christie Hosp.	Lady Marre	1979
The organisation and facilities at Rampton Hospital	Sir John Boynton	1980
The proposed closure of Cowley Road Hosp. Oxford	Prof. A.J. Willcocks	1979
Local Government in Scotland	Rt Hon. A. Stodart	1981
Chancery Division	Hon. Lord Justice Oliver	1981
A Heritage for Scotland	Dr Alwyn Williams DSc	1981
Committee of Inquiry into Angling in N. Ireland	Prof. R.D.C. Black	1981
Education for all: the report of the Committee of Inquiry into the Education of Children from Ethnic Minority Groups. 1979	Mr A. Rampton/Lord Swann	1985

1980

Committee of Inquiry into Offshore Safety	Dr J.H. Burgoyne	1980
The Value of Pensions	Sir Bernard Scott	1981
Non-accidental death of Paul Brown	Michael Morland QC	1980
The Enforcement Powers of the Revenue Depts. (Jointly with Customs	Lord Keith of Kinkel	1980

COMMITTEE	CHAIRMAN	FINISH

1981

Prevention of Fraud (Investors)		
Review Committee	Prof. L.C.B. Gower	1984
Arrangements for the Admin-		
istration of Sheriffdoms	Hon. Lord Grieve VRD	1982
Chain of Command: The Open		
Structure	Sir Geoffrey Wardale	1981
Civil Service Pay	Rt Hon. Sir John Megaw	1982

1982

Independent Review of the Radio		
Spectrum (30-960 mhz)	Dr J.H.H. Merriman	1983
Review of the National Assoc-		
iation of the Citizens		
Advice Bureauz	Sir Douglas Lovelock	1983
Regulation of British Telecom's		
Profitability	Prof. Stephen Littlechild	1983
Pedestrian Safety at Public		
Road Level Crossings	Mrs Sally Oppenheim	1983
Review of Railway Finances	Sir David Serpell	1982
Functions and Powers of the		
Islands Councils of		
Scotland	Sir David Montgomery	1984
Inquiry into Cable Expansion		
and Broadcasting Policy	Lord Hunt of Tanworth	1982
Falklands Islands Review	Lord Franks	1983
The Protection of Military		
Information. Report of the		
Study Group on Censor-		
ship	Gen. Sir Hugh Beach	1983
Selection of Fast Stream		
Graduate Entrants to the		
Home Civil Service, the		
Diplomatic Service and the		
Tax Inspectorate and of		
candidates from within		
the Service	Sir Alec Atkinson	1983
Committee of Inquiry into		
Children's Homes and Young		
Persons' Hostels (NI)	Mr Stephen McGonagle	1982

102

COMMITTEE	CHAIRMAN	FINISH
1983		
Review of the operation of the N. Ireland (Emergency Provisions) Act 1978	Sir George Baker	1984
Report of an Inquiry by HM Chief Inspector of Prisons into the security arrangements at HM Prison Maze relative to the escape on Sunday 25 September 1983, including relevant recommendations for the improvements of security at HM Prison Maze	Sir James Hennessy	1984
Report of the Committee on Professional Legal Studies (NI)	Prof. P.M. Bromley	1985
Matrimonial Causes Procedure	Hon. Mrs Justice Booth	1983
Inquiry into Proposals to Amend the Shops Acts	Robin Auld QC	1984
1984		
Committee on the Metra-Logical Control of Equipment for Use for Trade	E.N. Eden	1985
Bonnybridge/Denny Morbidity Review	Prof. L.H.M. Lenihan	1985
Conveyancing: (a) by non-solicitors; (b) simplification	Prof. J.T. Farrand	1985
Fraud Trials (Commissioned by the Lord Chancellor and the Home Secretary)	Lord Roskill	-
The outbreak of food poisoning at Stanley Royd Hospital in August 1984	John Hugill QC	Continuing
The death of Michael Martin at Broadmoor Hospital	Miss Shirley Ritchie	Continuing

COMMITTEE	CHAIRMAN	FINISH
Disposal of Radioactive Waste in N Atlantic (in conjunction with MAFF and the TUC)	Prof. F.G.T. Holliday	1984
Review of Arrangements for Protecting the clients of Air Travel Organisers	Sir Peter Lane	1985
Review of Public Utilities Street Works Act	Prof. Michael Horne	1985
Committee of Inquiry into the Regional Medical Cardiology Centre at the Royal Victoria Hospital (NI)	Mr J.M. Benn CB MA LLD	1984
Committee of Inquiry into Children's Homes and Hostels (NI)	Judge William Hughes	Continuing
The Report of the Committee of Enquiry into the Academic Validation of Degree Courses in Public Sector Higher Education	Sir Norman Lindop	1985
System of Banking Supervision	Robin Leigh-Pemberton	1985

1985

Review of Road Traffic Law	Dr Peter North	-
Conduct of Local Authority Business	David Widdicombe QC	-
Handling of Geographic Information	Lord Chorley April	-

* After 1975 the lists to not include committees and commissions established by the Foreign and Commonwealth which, at the time of writing, had been unable to supply them.

APPENDIX TWO: NEW STARTS, 1945–85.

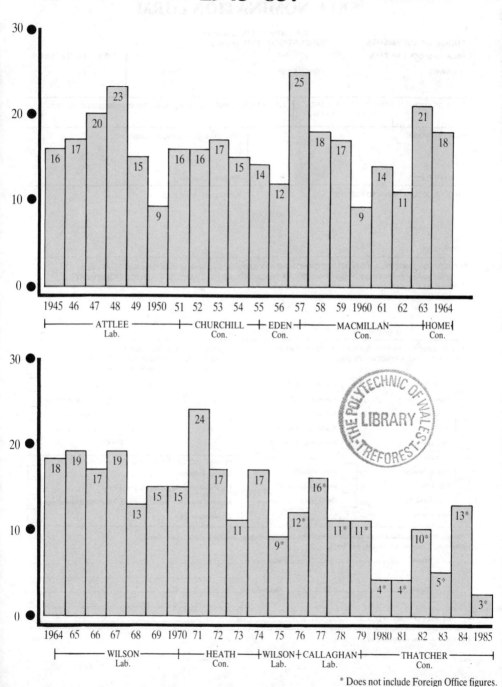

* Does not include Foreign Office figures.

APPENDIX THREE
CABINET OFFICE PUBLIC APPOINTMENTS UNIT
SELF-NOMINATION FORM

APPOINTMENTS IN CONFIDENCE

PUBLIC APPOINTMENTS: SELF NOMINATION FORM (PAN 3)

Please use BLOCK CAPITALS

FOR OFFICIAL USE

SURNAME	FORENAMES	TITLE

DATE OF BIRTH	MARRIED YES/NO	CHILDREN YES/NO	EDUCATIONAL/PROFESSIONAL QUALIFICATIONS/DECORATIONS

HOME ADDRESS	OFFICIAL OR BUSINESS ADDRESS
Telephone Number	Telephone Number
PRESENT OCCUPATION AND POSITION	PREVIOUS MAIN JOBS
Date taken up	

PREVIOUS OR EXISTING APPOINTMENTS OR VOLUNTARY SERVICE (eg Central or Local Government committees, charity professional, political or social committees) OR ANY BACKGROUND RELEVANT TO A PUBLIC APPOINTMENT (If more space is needed please use the reverse side of this form)

PLEASE INDICATE PARTICULAR AREAS OF INTEREST BY MARKING THE APPROPRIATE BOX

1	Agriculture	11	Construction
2	Food	12	Transport
3	Fisheries	13	Energy
4	Arts	14	Trade and Industry
5	Education	15	Finance/Economic
6	Consumer Affairs	16	Treatment of offenders
7	Health Services	17	Race relations
8	Social Services	18	Sex discrimination
9	Environment	19	Other (please give details overleaf)
10	New Towns		

PLEASE INDICATE THE AMOUNT OF TIME YOU WOULD BE ABLE TO MAKE AVAILABLE

Possibly full-time

Part Time   ½ - 1½ days per month

2 - 3½ days per month

1 - 1½ days per week

2 - 2½ days per week

More (   )

PLEASE INDICATE LOCATION OF WORK PREFERENCE

London Area only

Local area only (eg County Council area)

Regional Area (N.Ireland, Scotland, Wales, SE England etc)

Anywhere in UK

I confirm that I should like to be considered without commitment either way for a public appointment. References, if needed, can be obtained from:

1.   (Name) ....(Address) ....

....

2.   (Name) .... (Address) ....

....

Signature of Nominee .... Date ....

Please return when completed to:

PAN 3